PUBLIC
APOLOGY

PUBLIC APOLOGY

In Which a Man Grapples
with a Lifetime of Regret,
One Incident at a Time

DAVE BRY

GRAND CENTRAL
PUBLISHING

NEW YORK   BOSTON

Copyright © 2013 by Dave Bry

Some of these essays first appeared in modified form on the website The Awl (www.theawl.com).

A modified version of "Dear Asa" was previously published by the True/Slant blog network under the title "Death & Parenting."

"Born In the 50's"
Music and Lyrics by Sting
© 1978 G.M. Sumner
Administered by EMI MUSIC PUBLISHING LIMITED
All Rights Reserved International Copyright Secured Used by Permission
Reprinted by Permission of Hal Leonard Corporation

Grand Central Publishing
Hachette Book Group
237 Park Avenue
New York, NY 10017

www.HachetteBookGroup.com

Printed in the United States of America

RRD-C

First Edition: March 2013
10 9 8 7 6 5 4 3 2 1

Grand Central Publishing is a division of Hachette Book Group, Inc.
The Grand Central Publishing name and logo is a trademark of Hachette Book Group, Inc.

The Hachette Speakers Bureau provides a wide range of authors for speaking events. To find out more, go to www.hachettespeakersbureau.com or call (866) 376-6591.

Library of Congress Control Number: 2012949751

ISBN 978-1-4555-0916-4

For Mom and Deb

PUBLIC
APOLOGY

JUNIOR HIGH

(Or a time in my life that might best be rendered as one long apology to everyone I came into contact with. And also to myself.)

Dear Mike Eovino and Wally Rapp,

Sorry for offering you fake drugs in the boys' room at Markham Place Middle School.

It was not a nice thing to do.

The idea had come to me the day before, after a conversation we'd had—you two and Jeff Cadman and I—on the bus ride home from a class trip. I forget where we had gone. Was it the time we went to see the Shakespeare play at the Garden State Arts Center? *A Midsummer Night's Dream*, I think, but I didn't understand any of it.

Sitting in the seats behind you, Jeff and I had been talking about what everyone in Markham Place Middle School was talking about that day: the party that had taken place the previous weekend at Chloe Jessop's house, when Chloe Jessop's parents were not there. We had only heard about the party, of course. Chloe was a year older than us and pretty and popular in a way that assured that, even if we had been in her grade, we would not have been invited to her party. I would bet that Chloe Jessop didn't even know our names. We were all dorks, Jeff and I and you two, too. You'll remember, I'm sure, how far toward the front of the bus we were sitting that day.

Somehow, though, you came under the mistaken belief

that Jeff and I had in fact attended the party; the truth gar-
bled like in a game of telephone. Things that we had only
heard had happened at the party—drinking, make-out sessions, possibly even some pot smoking—you thought we
were discussing firsthand. Your eyes peeked back at us
through the space between the seats as you eavesdropped.
Then your heads popped up over the top as you knelt up and
turned fully around.

"You guys were there?!"

It was a pretty long bus ride. Jeff and I didn't have anything
better to do, so we lied.

"Yeah," I said. "It was wild!"

"Really?"

"Oh, man," Jeff said, laughing in a way that I thought
would sink us. "It was awesome!"

But you guys must have been as eager to hear a good story
as we were to tell one, because your eyes only lit up brighter.

"Did you guys, like, get drunk?" you, Mike, said.

I said yes. Though I had never gotten drunk in my life.

You were amazed. So I pretended to be amazed at your
amazement. "You guys have never gotten drunk?"

You had not. Wally, you mentioned that your dad drank
beer and that you'd seen him get "pretty tipsy," as you put it,
and that that was funny. (I remember your dad as being a particularly nice guy actually. He was an assistant soccer coach
when we were on the Wolves, right? In fifth or sixth grade?
Tell him hello from me.)

"Oh, man," I said. "It's the best! Right, Jeff?"

Jeff agreed.

Then we told stories about the party, going into great detail about the wildness and the craziness of all the debauchery we were imagining in our minds. Most of my details were coming from rock star biographies I'd read: *No One Here Gets Out Alive*, *'Scuse Me While I Kiss the Sky*, *Hammer of the Gods*. Pure fantasy, as far removed from my life as it was from yours. But you were buying it. So I kept on.

"You've never gotten a blow job?" Again, like I couldn't believe it.

Here's how laughable it was for me to be recounting sexual exploits at that time in my life: do you remember the episode of the TV show *Cheers* when Diane helps Sam write his memoirs, and Dick Cavett reads it and tells them that they need to spice it up with more salacious material about Sam's playboy days because sex sells, and so Sam and Diane go back into Sam's office to work on revisions and a little while later Diane comes out to the bar and asks Coach for a glass of water, but instead of drinking it she splashes it on her face and says, "Boy, can I write!" Well, that bus ride was bumpy, as bus rides always are, and my blue jeans were snug fitting, as blue jeans in the early '80s always were—as embarrassing as this is to admit, I had to cut short my graphic telling of a fictional seven-minutes-in-heaven session for the same reason that Diane needed a glass of water. Boy, could I write.

"You've never gotten high?"

Jeff and I debated our earlier assertion. Maybe getting

high was actually better than getting drunk. And which was the best drug? Pot? Speed? Cocaine? LSD? There were so many drugs we'd never tried that we told you we had tried, it was hard to choose a favorite. We had fun talking about it, though. And you seemed to be having fun listening, too. This was one of the most enjoyable bus rides home from a class trip any of us had had, I'm pretty sure.

So after it ended, after we got back to school, after school let out that day, Jeff and I decided to keep the fun going. We came up with a plan to turn our successful ruse into a more tangible prank. We went back to his house and spent the afternoon making fake drugs, which we would then present to you in a display of the peer pressure we'd learned about from ABC Afterschool Specials and when Nancy Reagan was on *Diff'rent Strokes*.

Standing by the sink in the Cadmans' kitchen, we spread out our materials on a tray: oregano, baking soda, the kind of ice-cream sprinkles that were tiny round balls of all different colors, Extra Strength Tylenol capsules, tinfoil, and Jeff's stepfather's rolling papers. (He rolled tobacco in them. But thinking back to the groovy John Lennon glasses frames he wore and the enthusiasm with which he showed me his original-pressing vinyl copy of Blind Faith's *Blind Faith* one night when I slept over there, I wouldn't be surprised to learn that if we'd looked around that house with any serious intent, we might have found some real pot to go with our oregano. Which would have probably freaked us out and ruined our whole gag.)

There was a window above the sink, and I imagined Jeff's neighbors looking in and seeing us rolling oregano into a cigarette, and folding the baking soda into a tinfoil envelope, and twisting the Tylenol capsules apart and dumping out the yellowish powder and replacing it with the sprinkles—which looked somehow "druggier" to us, more like a picture you'd see on a poster in the nurse's office—and sealing them back up with some spit. This would be a stupid thing to have to explain to the police.

I put the product in a sandwich baggie and hid it in the outside pocket of my knapsack. The next morning at school, Jeff and I coaxed you guys into the boys' room between classes. We didn't know what your reaction would be. Would you fall for it? Would you freak out? Would you tell the teachers? Would you take it? That seemed very unlikely, but hey, we didn't know. Who knows anybody that well, especially in seventh grade? And we'd all heard so much about the irresistible, almost demonic power of peer pressure. I hoped that you'd take some and then experience a placebo effect and start acting all funny, whereupon we would have the chance to say, "Ha-ha—you can't be feeling anything, it's fake!" I was prepared to swallow one of the sprinkle pills in front of you as encouragement.

"You guys are cool, right?" I said, checking the door to the bathroom over my shoulder. You looked suspicious but nodded a yes.

I pulled the stuff out of my knapsack. I took the joint out of the bag and held it out in front of me in my palm. Jeff opened the tinfoil to show you the white powder inside and presented the pills in a plastic bag. We'd done an impressive job. Everything looked very realistic.

Your eyes bugged, and you stiffened and took a step backward and stammered a refusal.

"No, no, no," you said, Mike, holding your hands out in front of you like this was a stickup. "No."

You giggled nervously, Wally, and moved to make an escape. "I…I…I gotta get out of here."

This was the same boys' room where Bobby Spano and Joey Figliolia used to pin me to the wall and call me "faggot" and muss up the hair that I'd been trying so hard to comb back in place every day after being out in the wind during lunchtime recess. I was tiny, and my hair was a curly mop, naturally all over the place, but I liked to grow it long because of Jim Morrison. But I also liked (or "desperately needed" is perhaps a more accurate phrase) for it to look *just so* if I was to be seen by any other people. Because of being in seventh grade. I hated that place a lot. That bathroom, Markham Place, seventh grade, all of it.

My miserableness, I would think, is what led me to play such a mean-spirited trick on you guys. "Shit runs downhill," my father used to say when I'd talk to him about bigger kids picking on me. He'd speak in a tone that acknowledged the sad unfairness of the world, but one that implied sympathy for the bullies, too. Maybe they had older brothers, he suggested, or mean parents who pushed them around at home. I don't mean to excuse myself by saying this. And I'd guess you'd know it already. But it's generally true, right? People who pick on other people have probably been picked on themselves. Bobby Spano took pleasure in seeing me scared in that bathroom—I tried to be as tough as I could, but he was way bigger than me and regularly twisted my arm behind my back until tears filled my eyes and I whimpered some sort of "uncle." I, in turn, reveled in the looks on your faces, your widened eyes and quivering lips, as you backed away from the joint I was offering you. Reveled in the little bit of power I had found.

"Come on, just try it," I said, mimicking the villainous, bad influencers from all the "Just Say No" commercials. "It'll make you *feel good.*"

I was awful.

You pushed past us and hustled out of there. Jeff and I laughed and congratulated each other, but it was halfhearted, anticlimactic. The prank itself paled in comparison to the process of setting it up. What were we supposed to do now, with these extremely lifelike fake drugs we'd spent so much time and care in preparing? And what did it say about us that we'd spent so much time and care in preparing fake drugs just to play a trick on you? We looked at each other warily and walked back into the hallway, off to our next class.

■ ■ ■

Dear Owner of a Bistro in Paris,

Sorry for spitting a mouthful of hamburger back onto my plate in front of your other customers.

This was the summer of 1983. I was sitting at a table in your restaurant with my father. We had come to Paris with his parents, my grandparents, on our way to Berlin, where we were going to see where they had lived before leaving Germany during the Holocaust. Like a *Roots* thing. My grandparents were Jewish.

I was twelve years old, which is a weird age to take a trip with your father. (It's probably more accurate just to say that twelve is a weird age.) On the one hand, it was wonderful. Flying in an airplane, staying in a hotel, seeing the different architecture and fashion, it was all like a movie—which is how you want everything to feel when you're twelve, or at least I did. This trip was even more special because we'd left my mom and five-year-old sister back home in New Jersey. My father sent me down to the *boulangerie* every morning, by myself, to buy us a baguette and cheese. "*Fromage*," I practiced saying, rolling the *r*, and made sure to count the change carefully.

At the same time, there was a lot of push and pull between me and my father that summer. Our relationship, which had always been very warm and pal to pal, was changing. Rock 'n' roll had replaced baseball as my principal obsession; I had recently come to an understanding of the notion of coolness and that this ran counter to enjoying time spent with one's family. And cool was something I very much wanted to be.

So Paris was a week of sightseeing and museums and walking around with a vague awareness of being in an in-between state as a person. I remember being bored, and complaining about being bored, and wishing that I could just stay in the hotel and work on lists in the spiral notebook I'd brought, wherein I obsessively ranked and erased and reranked again the things that were important to me: rock groups, rock songs, rock albums, singers, guitarists, drummers, bass players. Even Jim Morrison's grave, which we visited on my insistence, was a disappointment. It looked pretty much like all the other graves in the cemetery—just with some graffiti and a little two-foot-tall statue of his head. I was expecting something more along the lines of the Lincoln Memorial or the Statue of Liberty.

But the buzz and excitement of Paris at night! It really is a beautiful city. I can see why you've chosen to live in it. After my grandparents had gone to bed, my father took me out walking to look at the lights and the cars and the glamorous people in fancy clothes. I felt very grown-up and cosmopolitan. Swashbuckling even. Like we were a pair of playboys out on the town, staying up late, cruising the streets. We came upon a building with a façade of red panels with silhouettes of naked ladies on them—like the mud flaps behind the back wheels of eighteen-wheeler trucks. My father noticed me looking at them. "The world-famous Crazy Horse Saloon," he told me, with a devilish, man-to-man sort of wink. "It's a strip club."

I'm not sure why this struck me like it did. The year before,

11

he'd taken me to see *Porky's*, the first R-rated movie I'd ever seen, and a very dirty one, filled with nudity. And we'd enjoyed it; we had repeated the jokes to each other for months afterward. (Especially the one where the guys are at the diner, being interrogated by the police because one of them, the big football player named Meat, is drunk, and they're all lying to protect him—"No, no! He's not drunk! He's just tired!"—until the policeman threatens to arrest anyone who doesn't tell him the truth, and so they all immediately turn rat, and the little guy, Pee Wee, blurts out an overly enthusiastic, "The son of a bitch does it all the time!" We really liked that joke.) But as I said, my relationship with my father was changing that summer, and at that moment, out front of the Crazy Horse, realizing that just beyond that door there were women, real live women, on a stage with no clothes on, I felt a twist in my stomach and suddenly much less okay about being there with him. Swashbuckling with one's father is not swashbuckling at all. I stepped away to put more distance between us on the sidewalk. There could have been no sidewalk wide enough.

The next night, on a dark, crowded, stone-paved path that spiraled down a big hill where we'd gone to see the Basilique du Sacré Coeur after dinner, a strange man with a beard and foul breath lurched out of the shadows and grabbed me by the arm and said something loud and aggressive into my face in French. A quick blur later, before I'd even really registered what was happening, my father had grabbed the guy and slammed him against the wall on the side of the street hard enough that he crumpled to the ground. (The guy was likely headed in that direction already, drunk or drugged or both.) There was shouting and commotion and my grandparents hustled me away.

My father caught up to us a minute later. I don't remember exactly what my immediate reaction was. I don't think it was a major one. We walked back to the hotel like normal. I was perhaps experiencing some shock.

Later, in our room, as we were getting ready to go to bed, I pestered him into letting me turn on the TV. He'd said no at first—all the shows were in French; what was the point, other than to zone out? But eventually, he relented. I found a Japanese movie that looked interesting. A detective thriller, like a James Bond movie. A cool guy in a slick suit was searching an apartment for clues. Downstairs, we learned, an enormous thug—a sumo wrestler basically—was on his way to come kill him.

The thug burst in on the cool guy and there was a terrific, extremely violent fight. Furniture broke, glass shattered, the cool guy being beaten to a pulp. A bloody pulp. There was lots of blood. It was very graphic.

"Come on," my father said, putting his dopp kit back into his suitcase. "Why do you want to watch this?"

The fight spilled into the bathroom. The thug smashed the mirror with the cool guy's face. The cool guy fought back by stabbing the thug with something sharp and plugged into an electric socket. I can still remember the sound.

"This is sick, Dave," my father said. "Turn it off."

I didn't want to. I was riveted.

Then the thug grabbed the cool guy into a sumo-style choke hold. He was squeezing the air out of him, like a python. The cool guy's face, already so bruised and bleeding, puffed up and turned purple, started shaking and twitching. He was dying.

"This is gonna give you nightmares," my father said.

With his hands clawing the air, flailing around the bathroom counter in a last, desperate bid for life, the cool guy found a toothbrush. A red toothbrush with one of those '70s-era pointy rubber gum pick things at the end of the handle. And he took it in his fist and jammed it into the thug's ear. And he pushed it in hard and slow. The camera got a close-up. Dark, viscous blood, almost black, leaked out around the handle of the toothbrush, now buried three inches into the side of the thug's head. Now it was the thug who started twitching, and he released his grip on the cool guy and dropped dead. The cool guy left standing there, panting, had won.

I sat silent for a moment before I started screaming. I held my hands over my ears and buried my face in my pillow, trying to erase the image of the toothbrush sticking out of the thug's ear from my memory. It didn't work. I was screaming and sobbing and pulling at my hair. I squeezed my eyes tight but still saw it. It was all I could think of. The fat face twitching, the blood. It was overwhelming. It was as if I could feel that toothbrush stabbing into my own brain.

My father *tsk*ed and got up slowly to turn off the TV. He shook his head as he came over to the bed, and there was both scolding and sympathy in his voice when he said, "I told you not to watch that."

It must be a weird thing to go on a trip with your son when he's twelve.

Along with my horror was great shame over the fact that I was so horrified. Shame for crying in front of my father. Chagrin at such immediate proof that I had been wrong and he had been right. And I could tell that he was mad at himself, too. His tone softened when he sat down next to me. "I should have turned it off myself," he said.

I was in a panic. The television images flashing in my head, everything spinning and high-pitched and hot. It was very much like a nightmare actually, but one for which I was awake. I felt my father's hand on my back and pulled away and dug deeper under the covers.

It took him a long time to calm me down. I had lost any sense of control. I bawled and bawled and bawled and rambled in a hyperventilated stream of what I'm sure was mostly gibberish. But I know a repeated assertion that I didn't want to die was part of it. I don't know whether I connected this sudden mortal fear to what had happened with the stranger on the cobblestone path that night; I don't think I did. It's easier to in hindsight. I imagine it occurred to my father, though. He put his hands on my shoulders and forcefully turned me to face him.

"You don't have to be afraid," he said, looking in my eyes

and not blinking. "I'm never going to let anything happen to you. Do you understand? As long as I'm here, I will never let anyone hurt you. You or Mom or Debby. Never."

The next day, in retaliation for my father's protection and comfort when I was scared and crying and needing help, I sought even more distance from him on the sidewalks. In fact, when we went to the Louvre, I chose to stay outside in the topiary gardens while he and my grandparents went to look at the *Mona Lisa*. (The topiary was exquisitely manicured. Still, I now regret this decision, having never gotten back to the Louvre. I owe a separate apology to the museum's curator, or perhaps all artists everywhere, for so cavalierly passing up the only opportunity in my life so far to see the most famous painting on the planet.) The Louvre, I whined, was yet another in a long string of museums we'd been going to. Looking back, I'm pretty sure I just wanted some time alone. You can understand. And I'd bet my father did, too. He was a psychologist.

And then there we were at your bistro for lunch. A small place, six or seven other tables, most of them full. It was just me and my father at ours. I don't know where my grandparents were. We ordered burgers. My father had been exclaiming about the food in Paris all week. I don't remember appreciating it so much. I did like the cheese-and-butter sandwiches we'd make for breakfast every morning. And Orangina, I loved Orangina. Oh, and Nutella. Yum!

The burgers you brought us were super tender and juicy. I had my father, who spoke a little bit of French, ask for ketchup. But following his lead, thinking it very cosmopolitan, very *haute cuisine*, I put mustard on mine, too.

"This is delicious!" I told him after a few bites.

"Yeah?" He smiled. "I'm glad you like it."

"This might be the best burger I've ever had in my life!"

This time his smile was a little bit more to himself. "Good."

"What?" I said.

"Nothing. I'm glad you're enjoying it."

"What?" I pressed.

"Nothing," he said. "It's good, right?"

I was halfway through my burger and had a bite half-chewed in my mouth.

"Mmm-hmm."

"You know what it's made of?" he said.

I stopped chewing.

He told me. "It's horse meat."

I thought he was kidding at first, but quickly realized he was not. It turns out the French don't mind a little horse in their diet. I waited a moment and processed this new information and what I should do about it. Then loudly, exaggeratedly, I spit the food out of my mouth and onto my plate. *Pthew! Pthew! Pthew!*

"No!" my father whispered, angry and disappointed. "Come on! We're in a restaurant. Other people are here."

I wasn't really that disgusted. And really, why should I have been? I've never had any special relationship with horses. I wasn't a cowboy or a jockey. I'd ridden on a horse a handful of times—at fairs or farms or whatever. It wasn't like I'd been tricked into eating a pet. My dad was just trying to expand my horizons. Taking an opportunity to show me the limits of American provincialism. And sure, having a naughty little parental laugh while he was at it. He didn't think it would be such a big deal. But he'd underestimated my capacity for melodrama. The extent to which all of my behavior was beginning to be dictated by a notion of how I *ought* to be acting; how I might look to someone— someone like myself really in an out-of-body, mind's-eye perspective—sitting in a movie theater watching my life unreel on the big screen. Or reading about it in a trashy rock star biography. Or seeing it on TV in a sitcom. If Jack Tripper, say, or the Fonz were told that they were eating an animal that they didn't know they were eating, an animal that we didn't generally eat in America, that's what they would have done, coughed it up in a big, silly spit-take. That's what I imagined, at least.

I'm sorry if I caused a scene, or worse, cost you any business. Like I said, it had been a weird week. You want so badly to be cool when you're twelve. But sitting in a restaurant booth across from my dad in a foreign city famous for its strip clubs, two days after sobbing myself to sleep in his arms, I had a lot yet to learn about being cool.

■ ■ ■

PUBLIC APOLOGY

Dear Peter Arbour,

I'm sorry for insisting you worship my Jim Morrison poster.

This was when we were in sixth grade. You and Ted Trainor were over one afternoon. We were sitting upstairs in my room, bored, wondering what to do. Maybe it was raining outside. We were best friends, the three of us. We'd been so for years, through Indian Guides and Cub Scouts and carving weapons out of the bamboo that grew by the river, and sharing our first cigarettes in the fort we'd made at the base of the big walnut tree in your yard. My dad used to call us "The Three Amigos." And this was before that movie with Steve Martin and Chevy Chase and Martin Short.

But we were changing, as twelve-year-old boys do, and growing apart, at least in some ways. You and Ted were continuing with Boy Scouts. (You'd go on to become an Eagle Scout, I think. God, that's so much work, right?) I'd quit before making Tenderfoot. After the first campout, when we learned we were supposed to wash the higher-ranked Scouts' dishes after meals, I knew it wasn't for me. I was hanging out more with other friends, Chris Pack and Blair Bryan, and cultivating antisocial obsessions with Dungeons & Dragons and classic rock.

I had a poster of Jim Morrison in my room, tacked to the slatted door of my closet. It was that famous picture: bare chested, bead necklace, arms extended, Jesus Christ pose. "An American Poet," it said at the top. He was staring right at the camera, so the eyes seemed to follow you wherever you went. Chris and Blair and I attached a metaphysical significance to this and took to bowing our heads whenever we looked at it, intoning a reverential "*Jiiiiiimmm*" in order to ward off, I don't know, evil lizard spirits or something. "Indians scattered on dawn's highway, bleeding" and all. "Ghosts crowd the young child's fragile, eggshell mind..." (They'll do that, won't they?)

Understandably, when I explained the situation, that you'd entered the lair of a fervid geek cult, you and Ted refused to play along. I must have looked very weird, genuflecting before a poster of a dead rock star in my bedroom. You sneered. "He's not god, you know," I remember you saying. I insisted that yes, in fact, he was: those were the new house rules. You took a balled-up pair of socks that was lying on the floor and threw it to prove a point. You hit Jim right in the face, and it dented the paper there. Not a full rip, fixable with Scotch tape on the backside, but noticeable if you looked close. A moment later you and I were standing up, nose to nose. I was cursing at you; you were telling me again that it was just a poster. My cheeks were hot, and I remember the disdain in the way you looked at me. I shoved you and told you to get out. You didn't shove me back, and maybe that said more than anything else about where we'd found ourselves. We'd fought many times over the years. We'd had some of the most vicious fistfights I've ever had in my life. Remember the time on the dock at that boat club on the Navesink River where our parents were making us take sailing lessons?

Must have been the summer before—remember how much we hated those lessons? It was disgustingly hot, and we were in foul moods, the both of us, and I was drinking from your water bottle without permission, and you told me to stop and I didn't stop and you hit me (well, nudged me) with an oar, and then I did stop, and we traded punches until your glasses fell into the water. That ended the fight because we knew we would be getting in trouble, the both of us. Which we did.

But that day at my house, you and Ted just left.

A couple months later, I would fail Ms. Mawson's English class for refusing to write my final paper. We were all supposed to write a biographical report on a person of our choosing. I'd chosen, of course, Jim Morrison. (I'd memorized and recited the lyrics to "Not to Touch the Earth" for an earlier assignment.) Like you, I'd been an A student up to that point. (Technically, I guess, we'd been O students, since for whatever reason, Little Silver Schools chose Outstanding to represent the highest mark on our report cards, first grade through fifth.) But after reading *No One Here Gets Out Alive* as source material for the paper on Jim Morrison, I decided that the truest way to honor my subject was to not write anything at all.

"Jim wouldn't do homework," I told my dad, who grounded me for two weeks. In a strange way, I savored the punishment. I felt that not doing what I was supposed to be doing was exactly what I was supposed to be doing.

Adolescent rebellion is natural and healthy. Blind idol worship is not. You were right to throw those socks. Besides,

21

as great a rock star as Jim Morrison might have been, his po-
etry sucked.

■ ■ ■

Dear Wendy Metzger,

I'm sorry for singing the last verse of "Stairway to
Heaven" into your ear while we were slow dancing.

We were in the Markham Place gym, getting toward the
end of our first official school dance. I hadn't danced with
anyone up to the moment you approached me. I was a dork,
you'll remember. I had braces and a big pouf of red hair and
wore flood-ready jeans and the exact same type of off-white
baseball T-shirt with three-quarter-length navy-blue sleeves
every day. (I had six of them.) And a gray Members Only
jacket, much like the ones worn by my dork friends Jeff Cadman, Peter Arbour, and Chris Bruno. I'd spent most of that
evening standing in a tight circle with those guys, air gui-
taring to "Beat It" and "White Wedding." Thank god it was
dark in that gym.

We all stole glances at Mark McCarthy making out with
Suzie Lambert—right there in front of everyone, right in the
middle of the floor. Mark was in our grade, but Suzie Lambert was an eighth grader, a very pretty and developed one.
Mark's eyes were closed, but I'm sure he knew everyone was
watching him. I wondered what he must have been think-

ing, how much like a champion he must have felt. It was like looking at a taller, different, cooler species of human. How must someone's brain have worked to allow for something like that to happen?

I'm sure my friends tittered when you walked up and tapped me on the shoulder. But you seemed way more confident than any of us did. You smiled when you asked me to dance, hamming up a Sadie Hawkins–style formality. I'm sure I made some joke for my friends' benefit, but I was very happy to say yes, happy to be the one walking away with a girl.

I don't know what song we danced to first. "Little Red Corvette"? Probably not; I doubt I could have made it through the part about having a pocketful of "Trojans, some of them used" in that situation. "Every Breath You Take" was it? Or "Faithfully"? I know it was a slow song, because I was acutely aware of how close our pelvises were, and I was having a very hard time figuring how high or low on your back my hands should go. You talked to me nicely—we were getting to be friends in Mrs. Gill's science class—and by the end of the song, I was comfortable enough to ask you to dance again.

The lights blinked on for a moment, last call, and then the gentle notes started up and the flute, as familiar to me as my own name. I knew I was in trouble. It was "Stairway to Heaven," the live version from *The Song Remains The Same* album. I *loved* this song. I *loved* Led Zeppelin and was regularly thrown into spasms of unabashed ecstasy at the sound of their music. As far as I was concerned, "Stairway to Heaven" was the greatest song ever written, the single greatest piece of art ever created, the pinnacle of human cultural achievement. How would I keep my composure?

Not so well, as it turned out.

I did all right at the start, holding you closer than I had before. "This is an awesome song," I whispered. Surely you agreed. Everyone knew it. The music teacher, Mrs. Bloomberg, let us sing it in music class.

But as considerate as it was of the DJ to play it as the last song because it was ten minutes and fifteen seconds long (we would come to learn that it was played as the last song at each and every school dance), "Stairway to Heaven" is a terrible song to dance to. It gathers in tempo and heaviness as it goes along, and you don't know how to keep swaying, locked in an awkward twelve-year-old embrace, through the changes. (Mark and Suzie weren't having any difficulty, I noticed. They weren't even swaying really. And both Mark's hands were on her butt.)

A little after the halfway point, when the drums had kicked in, I was fingering imaginary double-neck guitar riffs on your dress. Softly enough, I hoped, that you wouldn't feel them. But you probably did anyway. "The piper's calling you to join him," Robert Plant sang, and a couple of minutes later, by the end of Jimmy Page's solo, the song in full stomp, I was helpless. I knew I was going to sing the last verse. It wasn't quite an uncontrollable urge. Almost. But it also had to do with holding on to what was my strongest sense of

24

identity at that point. I was a Zeppelin fan. A rocker, even if only in my mind. I *always* sang along with this song. Usually in a full-throated scream, drowned out by the speakers in my room. It felt like I'd be breaking some kind of promise to myself if I didn't sing the words I knew by heart.

So, unlucky you, out they came. "And as we wind on down the road…" Had my voice changed yet? I don't remember. But I'm guessing whatever adenoidal falsetto I mustered up didn't sound quite as polished as Robert Plant's professional pipes. It must have seemed very strange. Did you wonder if I was singing to you, like a serenade? Or whether there might be something wrong with me? Or with most boys our age? Perhaps you were impressed? That I knew all the lyrics? Or you thought how attractively uninhibited I was for singing along when the spirit struck me? That's hard to imagine, knowing how I felt back then, and how I felt like I looked, and how much I thought about that. I could never have come off as uninhibited. More likely, you were just confused. I would have been if I were you. I was confused and I was me.

Jesus, thinking back, what a performance it must have been! All the way to the end. That last line is so comically melodramatic in hindsight, stretching *buying* and *stairway* into three-syllable words. Sorry again. You must have been relieved when it was over.

A part of me was relieved, too. But another part of me would have stayed there dancing with you all night. Your hair smelled like shampoo.

■ ■ ■

Dear Australian Lady Guitarist Who Was a Counselor at Hidden Valley Camp, Summer 1984,

Sorry I never learned to play Neil Young's "Old Man" on guitar.

If there was one thing I hoped to do when I went to sleep-away camp, it was learn how to play the guitar. At the start of the summer, I'd gone to Jack's Music Shoppe and picked out a bunch of concert T-shirts—Pink Floyd, Rush, the Scorpions, Def Leppard—to wear with the OP shorts I'd bought with my mom at the mall. (Jack's, in Red Bank, New Jersey, would later become sort of famous, as the movie director Kevin Smith, who'd also grown up nearby, would have Ben Affleck's character live in an apartment directly above it in *Chasing Amy*. I spent hours and hours and hours there as a kid.) I hoped to present a new, cooler version of myself at camp. Camp's good for that. You can be anybody.

It worked almost immediately. The day I arrived at camp, after the lonely, nervous, eight-hour bus ride up to Freedom, Maine, and the boring welcome speech from the camp director, and not knowing who to stand next to for the opening-day group photo, which was taken with a special type of camera that rolled on a dolly so it was important that you stand absolutely still for an excruciatingly long time or you'd make a blur and mess up the whole thing for all the other two hundred people who were standing still along with you, the first friendly exchange I had was with one of the counselors assigned to my cabin, an English guy with a faint blond mustache—Andrew, I think his name was; do you remember him?—who complimented me on the shirt I was wearing. It was the Scorpions one, which had three-quarter-length sleeves and the picture from the cover to their *Blackout* album, which had come out in 1982.

"Cool shirt," he said as I was unpacking my duffel bag into my cubby. (This is funny to think about if you know what the cover of the *Blackout* album looks like. It's a picture of a guy screaming because he has forks stuck into his eyes. The Scorpions are a heavy metal band from Germany.)

"You like the Scorps?" I said. (I'd heard a radio DJ once talk about how all real Scorpions fans called the band the Scorps. Like you'd never hear anybody say, "The Scorpions rule!" It was always, "Scorps rule!" I henceforth referred to them only as the Scorps.)

"Yeah, they're all right," he said. "Good band."

"They rule," I said, suppressing the urge to qualify the statement by explaining how the Scorpions ruled slightly more than Golden Earring or Saga or Krokus in my estimation, but slightly less than Rush or the Who or Zeppelin. Also suppressing a smile because I had braces. And I was trying to be cool. But still, it was a big moment for me. Andrew must have been eighteen or nineteen or even twenty.

I suppose that's about how old you were that summer, too. Though to me, at the time, all camp counselors seemed like full-grown, super-secure, and comfortable adults who knew everything. I remember in particular how you would tuck your acoustic guitar under your right breast at the start of every lesson my bunkmate Chad and I signed up to take with you. Like it was nothing, like you didn't even notice doing it, sitting on a tree trunk stool in the little camper-built lean-to gazebo thing we'd use for shade. While I tried and failed not to stare. You had pretty large breasts. I was thirteen.

The goal of the lessons, which were the first such lessons either Chad or I had ever taken, was to be able to play a single song, Neil Young's "Old Man," by the end of the summer. We were supposed to play it in front of the rest of the camp at a commencement ceremony talent show.

It's a great song, "Old Man," and you taught us the lyrics, which are about youth and aging and loneliness and perspective. It's hard to learn to play the guitar, though. Harder than I'd thought it would be. The camp provided guitars for Chad and me to practice with; you'd said we should sit in the lean-to for an hour a day and go over whatever chord you'd taught us in the previous lesson. But I could barely reach my fingers around the guitar's neck; forming even a single chord that sounded like any of the ones you strummed seemed like an absolute impossibility. There are six different chords in "Old Man."

So I went to the lean-to to practice like twice. Hidden Valley was a big camp, on hundreds of acres of property. There was a private lake with floating docks and canoes, tennis courts, a soccer field, a ropes course—even a corral where they kept llamas. As it turned out, there was much more fun stuff to do with an hour of free time than struggle one's fingers into the unnatural position required for an A major seventh. Sneaking off into the woods and making out with Wendy Siegler, for example.

Do you remember Wendy Siegler? I doubt it, unless she was one of the campers in your cabin. Which I don't think she was. But I can't be sure. I can't actually remember which cabin Wendy was in. The fourteen-year-old girls' cabin, I suppose; Wendy was a year older than I was. But it's strange, I don't have a mental image of her cabin. And you'd think I would have been there. Even if I was perhaps not allowed inside because of rules, I would have seen the outside, known where it was. It's funny what you remember and what you don't, right? Certain things about that camp come back as clear as photographs. My cabin was a log cabin right next to the ropes course set up in the pine trees. It had a slanted roof, and a second-story loft where the counselors, Andrew and Matt Weiss, slept, and the door was near a wide plate glass window looking out at the path past the tennis courts toward the main red farmhouse. Or the shanty-style hot tub deck, where Matt taught an elective called '60s Rock. *Taught* seems like a funny word for it; he'd play tapes on a giant boom box and talk to us about the music. (Man, you counselors must have smoked so much pot at that camp, huh?) But actually, it *was* teaching. And I learned a lot. I can remember exactly where I was standing when he told me the story of the time the reporters were asking Bob Dylan about the meaning of his protest songs and Dylan said, "I've always thought of myself more as a song-and-dance man." I could draw a picture of it on a piece of paper. Other things, though, are hazy. Where was the lake in relation to the llama pens? Other things, gone. Where was Wendy's cabin that summer? What did it look like?

There's a pretty good chance you wouldn't remember Wendy even if she was in your cabin, I bet. She was a shy, quiet, short girl with curly blonde hair cut into a pyramid shape above her shoulders. Sort of like Madonna's in the "Borderline" video. She had braces.

She was cute, though. And Matt Weiss told me that I should ask her out because she had told him she wanted a boyfriend. And he knew, I guess, that I wanted a girlfriend since my friends Chad and Fernando and Geoff had gotten girlfriends. He had mentioned me to her and she had seemed receptive, he said. So after the big soccer game—you remember how the soccer team played a game every summer against that other camp? I forget the name. And how we tied them that year, one to one, because Peter Martin scored that beautiful goal near the end of the game? That long, arcing shot from the right corner? You must. Everyone who was at Hidden Valley that summer must remember that. A few years ago—well, like fifteen years ago—I was out at a bar with some friends of mine from college, and there was this guy there, a friend of a friend of one of my friends, and he looked very familiar, and so I asked whether or not we might know each other. And he said that he was thinking the same thing.

To try to figure it out, we went through where we had grown up and gone to school and where we'd worked in the city, and finally he said, "Did you by any chance go to a camp in Maine called Hidden Valley?" That was it; it turned out he was in my cabin that summer. And as soon as we'd put together this small-world coincidence, the first thing he said to me was, "Peter Martin's goal!" It was a major big deal, Peter Martin's goal, and the fact that we played this other camp to a tie, because we had lost to them like thirty summers in a row, because they were an all-boy sports camp and we were a coed hippie camp that raised llamas and had girls playing on our soccer team. Well, I had played in that game, too. I hadn't played as well as Peter Martin. But I played fairly well. Despite being short and also slow and not particularly strong, I was actually pretty good at soccer at that point. I played the whole game at right fullback, defense, and I blocked a corner kick just in front of our goal with my head. (I don't imagine you remember that.) So at the end of the game, when those of us who had played were mobbed by the rest of our camp, and it was all cheering and smiles and hand slapping and hugs, when I saw Wendy Siegler, I gave her a kiss right there on the crowded field and asked her if she wanted to go out with me. She said yes. This remains the single most heroic moment of my entire life.

The next night after dinner, Wendy and I went for a walk in the woods and sat on a bridge that went over a stream and talked. And for the first time outside the auspices of a game of spin the bottle or truth or dare or seven minutes in heaven,

I kissed someone with my tongue. We kissed for a long time, taking breaks to breathe, and shift positions, and stare at each other and giggle. We both had braces. It was her first time kissing this way, too.

Walking back across the soccer field toward our cabins, we held hands and it was like the sky was staying as light as it was as late as it was just so we could get back to our cabins and not get in trouble. Like we were in our own magic bubble, and everything was made just for us.

"Wow."

"Wow."

"I've never really done that before."

"Neither have I."

I heard the grass swishing under my sneakers, but I had the distinct and very powerful sensation that my feet weren't touching the ground. I told her.

"It feels like I'm floating," I said, and my own voice sounded different, like it was coming from somewhere deeper in my head than usual, almost echoey. "It's like I'm literally walking on air."

"I know," she said, her voice sounding dazed in its own way—swept up in the same rush. "Me, too. I've never really felt like this before."

The feeling was very much like being on drugs. Though I wouldn't have known that then as I had never tried any drugs. The effect of endorphins, I guess. I hadn't the slightest sense of inhibition. Or nervousness. For the first time in years, I didn't feel nervous. It was as if giant fingers had tamped down inside me on a guitar string that had been quivering for as long as I could remember. Suddenly I was calm.

"Is this what love feels like?"

"Maybe it is."

"I can't believe it."

"I can't believe it."

Needless to say, we devoted the rest of that summer to finding opportunities to steal away and recapture that euphoria. We got caught plenty of times, off in the woods or lying in a hammock somewhere when we were supposed to be at dinner or a camp meeting or doing some activity like practicing guitar. We never got in too much trouble. The staff at the camp was cool; you guys must have been used to that stuff from thirteen- and fourteen-year-olds. In fact, the assistant director of the camp that summer was Jim Newman, a family friend who'd known my father since they were kids. (They'd gone to Hidden Valley together, actually, in the 1950s.) When word of my delinquency reached him, he took to scolding me, but gently, with half a smile and reminiscences of my father's similar exploits. He found us himself once, on a bench on the trail that led to the lake, and marched us back to the dining hall with a smirk that said, "Wait till I tell your dad about this." My heart swelled in my chest.

Remember on one of the last nights of summer, when there was a meteor shower, and the camp director let us all sleep out on the soccer field to watch? I'll certainly never forget it. There must have been 250 of us out there. We clustered off as we wanted to, my friends and I claiming a patch of grass as far away from any counselors as we could get. Wendy and I zipped our sleeping bags together.

We lay on our backs and looked up at more stars than I'd ever seen in one sky. You could see layers and strata, stars behind stars, the canopy making a dome above the treetops surrounding the field. It felt like we were in heaven, and we kissed a lot and cracked jokes with Chad and Claudia and Fernando and Becca and Geoff and Stephanie, who were lying nearby in the dark. Then the meteors started, brighter streaks of light appearing out of nowhere and shooting off in all different directions, a new one every few seconds, and we *ooh*ed and *aah*ed along with the rest of the chorus on the field. It was like a fireworks show. But as the hours passed, the frequency of flashes tapered off, and the stars faded, and the voices and laughter got quieter and quieter, until the sound of our own hoarse, increasingly heavy breathing was all we could hear.

We'd stopped kissing by then. Neither of us had said anything for a long time. Wendy had undone my shorts, and pulled down the elastic band of my underpants, and was rubbing me roughly, sometimes against the metal teeth of my open zipper. It didn't feel very good, but I wasn't about to stop her. Not even for the second it would have taken to adjust my clothes. I wasn't going to risk breaking whatever strange spell we were under that was allowing what was happening to be happening.

I had slid my hand slowly, tentatively, centimeter by centimeter, beneath the waistline of her sweatpants and that of her underwear, expecting to be stopped any second. But she didn't stop me and instead reciprocated, and now I was being granted tactile access to heretofore secret contours and textures: the tight, scratchy curls of hair; the slope of the firm but bulbous mound; the surprisingly vertical angle of entry. The wetness—different from, slicker than sweat.

Eventually, she withdrew her hand, and I withdrew mine, and with a soft, quick kiss on the lips, but still no words, we turned away from each other.

I had no idea what time it was. Midnight? Two a.m.? Four? It was pitch-dark, and in my excitement and lack of sleep, I'd entered a strange mental state. Hyperaware of certain sensations, I found myself disoriented and confused about other aspects of my situation. Which way were we laying? In what direction were our heads pointed? How far away were we from the woods? From our friends? From the nearest counselor? Was I still wearing my socks, or was that just the lining of the sleeping bag? And of course, part of me suspected that this was all just the luckiest dream anyone had ever dreamed.

So you understand, I'm sure. No matter how badly I wanted to learn to play the guitar that summer, no matter how good a teacher you were, or how cool and comfortable and easygoing, no matter how great a song "Old Man" is— and it is such a great song, and I think of you, sitting under that lean-to gazebo thing, every time I hear it, to this day— there were more powerful forces at work. We ended up not performing in front of the rest of the camp at the end-of-summer talent show.

Later that year, after I got home from camp and school started, I convinced my parents to buy me an electric guitar. I took lessons from a guy named Chaz at Red Bank Music for two years. But he couldn't make me practice, either. I made a lot of noise in my room, played with feedback, bashed out the riffs to "Smoke on the Water," and "Iron Man," and Neil's "Hey Hey, My My." But I never did learn how to make a proper chord.

■ ■ ■

Dear Mrs. and Mr. Carr,

Sorry for stealing a six-pack out of the fridge in your garage.

After all, you were nice enough to host a graduation party for our class at your house next to the Arbours' house on Point Road. Your daughter Tammy and I had just finished eighth grade, just graduated from Markham Place School together. We were supposed to sing John Lennon's "Imagine" at the ceremony, which was held by the gazebo on the hill by the baseball fields. Our music teacher, Mrs. Bloomberg, had taught us the words, playing along on her piano. But there was controversy: certain parents, or perhaps members of the administration, didn't like the part about imagining that there was no heaven and no religion. So we didn't sing it. We sang something else. "Climb Every Mountain," maybe?

Your party was a couple days later. I picked out my nicest shirt to wear, a white polo shirt that was probably not actually Polo, as I would have liked it to have been, but more likely just Izod and maybe even just Le Tigre—my parents, to their credit, having refused to spend large amounts of money on clothes that I would soon spill pizza sauce on.

You had a pool and a big long lawn sloping down to the reeds by the river, and you'd set up tables on the patio with chips and soda and a six-foot sub from Danny's. It was a warm June evening on the suburban Jersey shore and the air smelled like honeysuckle.

We were all super-psyched, Tammy and I and our classmates, having just gotten out of grade school forever. I had not enjoyed the past few years at Markham Place. I was not so popular. On one of the last days of school, when we all got our yearbooks and people started asking each other to sign them, I mustered up the courage to ask Liz Dilascia, one of the most popular girls in our class, to sign mine. "Dear David," she wrote, "I don't know you very well, but I know you're very nice! Have a great summer!" This made me wish I had not been able to muster up that courage. Not that that was Liz Dilascia's fault. She was just being honest. (What was she supposed to write, "Give me a call some time?") She didn't sneer when I asked or say, "Gag me with a spoon!" or anything like that. Our class had gone on an overnight trip to Washington, DC, a week or so before then—one that served to bring us together as a group more than I had expected. On the bus ride, in the hotel, at the Lincoln Memorial, and the US Mint, kids talked to and laughed with kids they hadn't talked to or laughed with through eight years of sharing a lunchroom. I guess everyone was really happy to be graduating.

Immediately after the ceremony at the gazebo, the school itself had thrown us a party in the gym of the lower-grades grade school, Point Road. There was a DJ and pizza and cake with pink frosting so sweet that it hurt your teeth. We all went crazy to Prince's "Let's Go Crazy" and shouted the "Hey! Get laid! Get fucked!" ad-lib parts we were supposed to shout when the DJ played Billy Idol's version of "Mony Mony." And we were moved to a level of genuine compassion and emotion that felt foreign to fourteen-year-olds when Martin Torbert, who was in a wheelchair because of the muscular dystrophy he would die from six years later, slow danced with his girlfriend to Survivor's "The Search Is Over." Then someone had the idea that Ted Trainor and Matt McCabe and Dave Murgio and I should do a lip sync performance of the Rolling Stones' "Start Me Up." Ted and Matt and Dave were all more popular than I was, but I was known as a music nut, and the Stones were my favorite band; this is the reason I was included. Dave and I argued for a minute over who would get to be Keith Richards, but since Dave was more popular, and since he said I would know the words better, he won and I agreed to be Mick Jagger.

I was a little nervous when the music started, looking out

at the faces of my classmates who I knew didn't know me very well and who I feared didn't like me very much. But everyone was smiling and obviously into it, so I got into it, too. I danced like Mick and put my hands on my hips and threw my arms back and stuck out my lips and pouted as I mouthed the words into the imaginary microphone I held in my hand. I had his moves memorized from watching the famous video of him singing this song onstage in the Philadelphia Eagles jersey during the Tattoo You tour from a few years before. I had practiced them plenty into the mirror in my bedroom. I strutted like a rooster and leaned back-to-back against Dave, just like Mick and Keith did, when we harmonized on the "You make a grown man cry-aye-aye" parts.

Everyone screamed and cheered and mobbed us at the end of the song, just like we were real rock stars, just like what I wanted most in the world to be. Well, they mobbed Ted and Matt and Dave more than they mobbed me. But as things settled down, and people went back to get a last slice of pizza or piece of cake with painfully sweet pink frosting, Liz Ryan, who was pretty and popular but also a bit shy, came up to me and smiled and quietly said, "You were a good Mick Jagger."

So I was feeling like a new and different kind of person as I walked out onto your pool patio in my white Le Tigre polo shirt. A better kind of person, one who stood up straighter and might have greeted people with a joke because he was not afraid they would think it stupid and laugh at him and not with him. In my ridiculous fourteen-year-old mind-set,

I saw myself on the verge of crossing over the imaginary but all-important line dividing my peer group into two clearly defined halves. The notion of popularity, the difference between being a loser and being cool, seems so vague in a quarter century's worth of retrospect. Such a thing must be fluid and open to various interpretations, right? But that line seemed so stark as I saw it. So unbending and so desperately crucial. It makes me sad to think about it now.

But that was my reality back then. And I remember breathing deep that night, walking out past the pool onto the grass and looking up into the sky and feeling like I was starting to get it a little more—the mysterious social codes that had flummoxed me for so long. It was nearing the end of the party, and I turned and saw all the kids in my class gathered on your patio, faces glowing in the lights mounted on the back of your house. It seemed like everyone was wearing white. Some of the girls had started dancing, which made me proud, because the music playing was a mix tape I'd brought. I'd made it special for the night and filled it with songs carefully chosen to make people like me more. *Party Songs!* I titled it. I included "Start Me Up," of course, to remind Liz Ryan and everyone else of how like Mick Jagger I was. "Let's Go Crazy" and "Mony Mony" were on there. And "Shout" from the toga-party scene in *Animal House* and the Romantics' "What I Like About You." And "I Heard It Through the Grapevine" and "Joy to the World." *The Big Chill* had come out that year, and its popularity felt a little like a conspiracy, carried out by those of your and my parents' generation, to get us kids to like your music and not listen to rap. (That's pretty much what it was, right?)

Soon after returning to the patio, I felt a tap on my shoulder. It was Jason Appio, who whispered that I should come with him. He'd found something I should see. We cut through the crowd and slipped through a back door that led into your garage. Waiting there, in the dark, huddled near a refrigerator against the house's side wall, were a few other guys from our class. Colin Dodds and Eddie Griffin, I think. Jerome Connelly and Mike Scaccia. All more popular than I was; but again, that was not a difficult status to attain. And I was catching up.

"Check this out," Jason said.

He looked around to make sure no one was coming and opened the refrigerator. A hushed buzz arose from the group. There was beer inside.

He closed it quickly, and we all stood there, bouncing on the soles of our feet. Jason looked at me. "What do you think?"

I knew what he meant. I knew why he had come and gotten me. Earlier that year, at Mindy Gallop's bat mitzvah at Temple B'nai Israel in Rumson, after the ceremony, while Mindy and her family stood in the receiving line outside the main sanctuary, and we were all left to mingle out by the tables spread with the cheese and grapes and crackers and wine they always had out in the lobby area, before heading to the reception, I had been the one to take a bottle and hide behind a couple taller boys and pour the little plastic shot glasses of

Manischewitz that counted, for me at least, and probably for Jason and a bunch of the rest of us, as our first non-adult-sanctioned sips of alcohol.

It wasn't really a question what any of us thought about your beer. We all wanted to take it, if only for the adventure. The question was who would be the thief.

The fridge was opened again; its interior light glowed in our faces. The six-pack beckoned. The sounds of the party, the nice party you were nice enough to throw for us all, came in muffled from the patio outside.

"Grab it."

"Grab it."

"*You* grab it."

I grabbed it. The fridge closed silently. We made a beeline to the door on the other side of the garage. I held the cans by the plastic rings that kept them together, held them as low against my leg as I could.

Outside, though, behind the bushes near your driveway, I held them up high for the other guys to see. Then I pulled them out of the packaging and handed them out. Booty, bounty, proof of my derring-do. I forget what kind of beer it was.

"I told you," Jason said to the others as we stifled our giggling and popped the tabs. I was catching up fast.

Of course, in retrospect, I was falling behind in some other ways. Important ways. My willingness to excuse myself of anything in the name of being cool and more popular, for example. I went into this knowingly and aware, accepting it on the principle that desperate times call for desperate measures. And that poor, jerky behavior was okay because I was a teenager and that's what I had read and heard and seen that teenagers did.

It's not the biggest deal in the world, I know. But I owe you a six-pack. I think I left that mix tape at your house, though. Maybe you still have it. Maybe you still listen to the Motown songs on there from *The Big Chill*. I hope you do.

■ ■ ■

Dear Matt Weiss,

Sorry for sneaking out of the cabin while you were asleep.

This was late in the summer of 1985, a week or so after the camp took that day-trip to the lobster docks on the coast, and you and I found a place with a TV that was broadcasting Live Aid and sat there and watched for a few hours and marveled that Phil Collins was actually flying, at supersonic speed, on the Concorde, across the Atlantic Ocean, to get stadiums full of people to do the big drum part to "In the Air Tonight" in London and Philadelphia on the same day. And how sludgy and out of tune Led Zeppelin sounded. Remember that?

We were both total music nuts. And good friends, in my eyes at least, despite our age difference—I was fourteen, you had just started college that year—and the fact that you were a counselor and I was a camper. I'd been in your cabin the previous summer. You and your friend Matt Palmer were widely regarded as the coolest counselors on the staff—this despite the fact that you wore Philadelphia Eagles jerseys and some sort of Greek tunic and sometimes a dashiki. Your favorite band was Jethro Tull. You had named our cabin Gonzo and decorated it with *Doonesbury* comic strips, with the explicit intent of introducing us to Hunter S. Thompson and New Journalism. I was so psyched to have been assigned to you again.

Late one night, during the first week of camp, you'd come in and woken me up with a flashlight. You were coming back from a night off, and you and a couple of the other counselors had gone into town, where you had bought a copy of a *National Lampoon* spoof of *Rolling Stone* magazine. You stepped up on the ladder of my bunk and opened the pages next to my pillow. "You've got to see this," you whispered, keeping quiet not to wake anyone else.

We read through the whole magazine, which you had already read through once before, holding our hands over our mouths to stifle our laughter. It was really funny. They had a fake interview with Jerry Garcia, where he said he was looking forward to taking part in the recording of "We Are the World" and asked the reporter if he knew when that was happening. The song had been out for months already, of course—an annoyingly ubiquitous worldwide smash that had gathered, for its making, pretty much every major American music star of the moment to the highest-profile recording session Hollywood had ever seen. The joke being that Jerry Garcia was too old and out of it to have been invited. And also too old and out of it to realize this.

"I had to wake you up," you said. "I knew you would appreciate this." I wonder if you knew how good it would feel for me to hear that, to know I'd been chosen as the one kid allowed to stay up late and share a private laugh with a counselor, especially a counselor as cool and universally beloved as you were. I think you might have.

I had been having a terrible start to that summer. Wendy Siegler had broken up with me on the very first day of camp. Immediately, not ten minutes after I'd stepped off the bus. My heart had fluttered when I found her face in the crowd that had gathered to greet new arrivals. I'd been waiting to see her for almost a year. But when I approached her, when I leaned in to give her a kiss, she stopped me and said we had to talk. We walked a short way over to a picnic table near a pine tree, and she smiled a weird smile. There were still plenty of people near us. "I'm breaking up with you," she said. Just like that.

I don't remember what I said. We talked only for a short time. She was cold and clipped with her words. And, in fact, seemed to be taking pleasure in them. Like she was acting out a scene she'd been practicing—and looking forward to. There was a gleam in her eye. I forget her reasoning, or whether she even offered any, and whether I argued or asked any questions. I tried hard not to cry as she walked away back to her friends, who had been watching.

The breakup came as a huge and brutal surprise to me. It shouldn't have, but it did. Wendy and I had stayed in touch over the phone since the summer before. (She lived in Manhattan.) For the first few months, our conversations bubbled with the giddy excitement of young love. We talked about the start of the school year—she had started high school, a big scary deal—and about mutual camp friends we'd heard from, letters we'd received. We told each other that we missed each other and made plans to try to see each other that never materialized. Still, it was great.

Simply having a real, live, actual girlfriend, even one that I never saw, counted as an important victory in my mind. Even if my success at camp didn't translate directly into coolness and higher social status at home (and, of course, it didn't), I could imagine now, if only just slightly, what it might feel like to be a popular guy like Mark McCarthy, making out with Suzie Lambert in front of everybody at the school dance.

On top of that, though, the pleasure of having a girlfriend was enhanced, as ridiculous as it seems now, by the fact that this particular girlfriend's name was Wendy. I attached profound metaphysical significance to this. Not because another girl I knew, a girl with whom I'd once danced at a school dance, was also named Wendy, Wendy Metzger. That was mere coincidence. Rather, it was because (and I'm sure you understand this) to a certain kind of classic-rock-radio-inundated person from New Jersey, one who has most of the lyrics to Bruce Springsteen's *Born to Run* album memorized, the name Wendy is synonymous with an idealized sort of romantic glory. If you are that kind of person from New Jersey, and you are thirteen years old, Wendy is a girl with whom you want to die on the street tonight in an everlasting kiss. And then you say, "*Chuh!*"

The fact that my first girlfriend's name was Wendy seemed like nothing short of destiny manifest. It was like Bruce was singing *my* story, and surely, Wendy and I were *meant* to be together. Unsurprisingly, such faith in rock 'n' roll fantasy occluded my view of the situation. As the year had passed, as summer faded into memory, and the pressures of the here and now took precedence, our conversations had become less frequent and more stilted. By that spring, the times when we did talk, Wendy sounded like a very different person than she had the summer before. (And who wouldn't? Considering her age and the fact that this was her freshman year of high school. And that I was still in eighth grade. Like Howard Jones said, in one of the highlights of Live Aid that we watched on TV that day at the lobster docks, "No one is to blame.") I know I noticed her blasé tone, her quickness to get off the phone. How much less friendly she'd become, how *much* less lovey-dovey. I was confused, but I chalked it up to the vast mystery of female behavior, of adolescent behavior or human behavior in general. To the vast mystery of the world. What did I understand about anything then? The system of signs and superstitions offered sparing revelation, brief glimpses of the truth. I clutched at what I believed to be fate and moved forward in blind hope. And, despite all the evidence pointing to the fact that I would not be needing them, bought a pack of condoms to bring to camp.

It didn't seem *that* outlandish, bringing condoms, considering where Wendy and I had left off the previous year. I certainly wouldn't have wanted to end up in a situation unprepared and have had a lack of planning—a simple $3.50 purchase or whatever a three-pack cost back then—impede an opportunity to achieve what had already become the single most anticipated event of my young life. The one thing that I prayed to god for. (To the extent to which I believed in god, which was not very much.) *Please, dear god*, I prayed. *If you do in fact exist, please, please, do not let me die without knowing what it feels like to have sex.*

Except that it was not at all a simple purchase. It was excruciating. The Saturday before leaving for camp, I rode my bike to Krauser's, our local pharmacy, and spent a very cliché-feeling half hour beneath the overbright neon lights, collecting a range of inventory I did not want or need, and making a pile on the counter at the cash register, before taking a deep breath and lowering my voice and asking the clerk would she please retrieve a packet of Trojans from where they were displayed on a rack behind her. I was expecting her to laugh in my face. ("Ha! These are for *you?*") But she didn't.

A couple hours later, after I'd gotten home and hidden the condoms inside a balled-up pair of socks at the bottom of the duffel bag I was packing, my father called me into his room.

"I got something for you to take with you to camp," he said.

I waited, and he opened up a brown paper bag. From a pharmacy.

"Your mother and I don't want you to be having sex yet," he said. "But I know you have a girlfriend you're going to see. And I know people are having sex at younger ages than they used to. And if you do have sex, I want you to be safe about it."

He pulled a different three-pack of condoms out of the bag and handed it me.

"Oh, god! Jeez, Dad!"

Mostly joking, buoyed by a wave of pride I hadn't expected, I scolded him, both for embarrassing me with this horrible issuance of responsible parenting and for not doing so earlier before I had blown thirty dollars in distractive purchases and suffered through the prior humiliation at Krauser's. He smiled. It was actually a nice moment.

So I had brought a total of six condoms to camp with me, in the hope that I might need them to keep from getting Wendy Siegler pregnant that summer. A hope that, once it was so decisively expunged, looked horribly, ridiculously hubristic in retrospect. ("Ha! Those were for *me*?") The image of the two unopened packets, hidden at the bottom of the duffel in the cubby, gave me an extra bit of pain those first couple nights of camp, a twinge of self-reflective pathos, as I lay sleepless in my sleeping bag on that top bunk in Gonzo cabin, feeling like I'd had my chest kicked in.

You were the only person I really talked to about it. I tightened my throat against tears as I told you—in an otherwise empty cabin; I'd feigned illness to skip out of some activity—about what had happened when I got off the bus. You had already heard. You knew Wendy. (You had introduced us the summer before. I'm sure you don't remember that. It's funny how a shared experience can be such an auxiliary blip in one person's life while accumulating such major narrative weight in the other person's.) And you knew her friends, and girls talk about these things. You said you'd told Wendy that she was being a bitch. But there was not a lot you could do except offer me sympathy and tell me a story of when you'd had your heart broken by a girl, too. And share a wincing smile when I confessed the story of the condoms. I appreciated your honesty. "It hurts," you said. "And the only thing that makes it better is time. But it eventually goes away."

You were right. And in the way that summer days can seem to encompass weeks, and weeks months, the heartache receded quickly, and I fell into the swing of soccer and swimming in the lake and, always a favorite part of my day, listening to records and talking about music with you and the six or seven other kids who'd signed up for your '60s Rock elective. In a session dedicated to Crosby, Stills, Nash & Young, you played us the song "Ohio" and told us the story of how it was recorded: in May 1970, two weeks after the army had shot four students protesting the Vietnam War at Kent State University. How Neil Young had brought a magazine article about the incident to the studio, with the famous image of the girl kneeling over the dead body. How David Crosby started crying as he was singing. You could hear it at the end of the song. "Why?" he wails. "Why?" We learned a lot in that elective.

My friends, too, helped make for a faster recovery. Chad had not come back that summer, but Fernando had from Spain and Geoff from California. And I'd made a new buddy, Jon, who was in our cabin. And the girls, too. Despite Wendy having dumped me, the core group of us from the summer before remained intact, so I stayed friends with Stephanie and Becca and Michelle, who was Jon's sister, and Christina, who was Fernando's sister and who was shy and didn't speak English so well, even though she was a year older, but was tan and blonde and radiantly beautiful, and would smile and laugh along with whatever was being said, sometimes with the help of a brotherly translation. Wendy was often around but didn't talk much to me. Soon enough, I didn't mind.

There was that one time, though, when I had a heavy whopping doozy of a freak-out. I would think you do remember this because I scared everybody and ended up sleeping in the infirmary for the night. I still don't know what happened for sure. Best as anyone could tell, I had some sort of psychotic episode; that's the way my parents always termed it afterward. They were both psychologists, my parents.

It was around the middle of summer, two or three weeks into camp. There was some social event in the dining hall. A movie or a dance party or something. And then a big bonfire by the lake. I don't remember exactly when I started to feel out of sorts. But at a certain point, around dusk I guess, as it started to get dark, I was gripped by the idea that I had to get away from the camp. I wanted to run away. To steal off to the road through the woods and hitch a ride somewhere, anywhere else. I don't have a strong sense of why, except that it had to do with the idea that we, the campers, the kids, were being imprisoned. That we needed to break for freedom. I remember being sickened by the sight of couples cuddling at the social, too. So I suppose the whole thing might have been a delayed symptom of my broken heart; but it didn't feel like that. I was angry, not sad. And Wendy was not in my thoughts at all, not consciously at least. Mostly, it was the notion of freedom. I repeated the word to myself, a weird mantra. I needed to get free.

I left the dining hall in a fever and stomped around by myself for a while, formulating a plan of escape. But I needed a partner. I was certainly not brave enough to walk off into the woods of Maine by myself. So I went down to the beach on the lake. The fire was burning high, and a crowd had gathered, sitting on the sand, and one of the counselors was leading a sing-along with an acoustic guitar. (Was it you? I don't think so. But you did play guitar, right? You used to play "Alice's Restaurant" on our bus trips. You knew the whole thing by heart, the whole rambling, thirty-five-minute story. Or did Matt Palmer play the guitar while you just led the singing?)

I saw Becca standing at the edge of the circle. I tapped her on the shoulder and told her I was thinking of running away and asked if she wanted to come. She looked slightly concerned—she was always so nice—but said no, she was en-

joying the bonfire. Jon, too, I asked. He thought I was joking.
We were jokers with each other, me and Jon. I walked away
and bumped into Geoff.

"Geoff! Thank god I found you."

"Hey, man. What's up?"

"We have to get out of here."

"What?"

"We gotta do something big. This place is bullshit!"

"Yeah. Umm..."

"This is bullshit! It's like jail here. We need to do something big to let them know they can't treat us like this. We
gotta get out of here."

"What do you mean?"

"Let's get out of here. We can sneak out to the road and
hitch a ride somewhere."

"Whoa, man. That sounds pretty crazy. I don't think we
want to do that."

"I don't care about getting in trouble! We need to do something big! Don't you want to be *free*?"

"Are you okay?"

I ran off and found a dark place under a tree with low,
wide-reaching branches. I could see the bonfire back from
where I'd come, a hundred yards away or so, and our cabin in
the other direction, through a grove of pines, a little farther.
I leaned my back against the tree trunk and stayed there for
a long time, thinking desperate, paranoid, lonely thoughts.
I didn't understand what was happening to me, but had the
strong feeling that I had seen some truth, discovered some-

thing corrupt and wrong with the world and that I had to do something big and momentous about it. To make some statement about youth and freedom and rebellion. But it was all so vague and confused. Very, very confused. It was all swirling in my brain. When I closed my eyes, I saw stars.

After a while, I saw everyone leaving the bonfire. People passed me on the way to their cabins. I stayed quiet and hidden. Soon after that, there was commotion, and I heard people calling my name. Flashlights. Your voice.

I came out from under the tree and heard someone shout, a kid, someone from our cabin. "There he is!" Then I fell flat on my face. Like a two-by-four. Without even knowing it. It was if the world just tipped to the side. One moment, I was standing on the patch of grass; the next moment the patch of grass was rushing up to meet my face. More shouting. "He fell!" People running toward me. "He fainted!" Your voice again. "Give him room! Give him air!" Then I was laughing hysterically. Then I was sobbing.

You lifted me up. You and one of the other kids. But I couldn't lock my knees. My legs were like Jell-O. I crumpled back down and kept crying.

You picked me up and put me over your shoulder and ran me across the central field to the infirmary. The camp director met us there—Jay, with the big gray beard—and a doctor. The lights were bright inside; it was a blond wood room, and I was lying on a padded table. I stopped crying, but I couldn't make sense of my thoughts for a while. I'm not sure if I could talk, or if I was talking, I'm not sure what I said. It might

have been gibberish. It was clear that you and the camp director and the doctor were very concerned. You spoke to me
very slowly. "Take deep breaths."

Dizzy and numb, I came back to myself after a while and
sat up. I wasn't in pain. My head was a little cloudy, but I
actually felt pretty good. I didn't feel like running away anymore or that the camp was an evil organization set up to
oppress kids.

The doctor asked me if I had taken any drugs. "No," I said.
I hadn't. Ever.

Had I ever had an epileptic seizure? "No."

They got my father on the phone and his voice sounded
strange. "David," he said, "I want you to tell me the truth:
Did you take any drugs tonight?"

I told him I hadn't. And we talked for a short time before
he got back on the phone with the doctor. I told him that
I was feeling better now. He'd later tell me this night had
been the most frightening night of his life. He'd had experience with psychological breakdowns before—professionally,
involving some of his clients—and he knew that sometimes
people freaked out and didn't ever come back. He said he almost got in the car and started the eight-hour drive up to
come get me. He didn't because the doctor confirmed that I
was getting better. But he said he didn't sleep anymore that
night. "It was terrible being so far away, not knowing what
was going on," he said. "I thought we might have lost you."

At the infirmary, drugs remained the main avenue of in-
quiry. Was I sure I hadn't taken any drugs? Might someone

have given me drugs without my knowing? Had I met and talked to a stranger? Had anyone given me anything to drink or eat?

"Oh," I said. "Yes, actually. John gave me a soda."

At the social in the dining hall. I had been sitting with a guy from our cabin named John. (Another John, not my jokeful buddy.) And he'd gotten up to get a soda, and—I forget whether he'd offered or I'd asked—he got me one, too. Either way, innocent enough. I had been friends with him the year before but less so that summer. He seemed surly a lot of the time. Or maybe just sad. Indeed, some people said he was into drugs. I didn't know. That was a pretty common assertion for people to make about someone who seemed surly or sad—we were of the age when drug taking generally started, and the blanket bogeyman description of someone being "on drugs" was something we were hearing a lot from daytime talk show hosts and the president's wife. I don't think John dosed me with anything. That would be weird to bring, say, a tab of acid out to a party and surreptitiously put it into someone else's soda. Crazier things have happened, I suppose. But for starters, if you were into acid and you had gone to the trouble of bringing acid to summer camp, giving acid to someone else without their knowing would be a waste of your acid, wouldn't it?

I spoke to John about it myself a couple days after it had happened. He said he didn't do it. And he didn't seem guilty or anything. But when I described to him how I'd felt that night, he said it sounded like someone had slipped me something. I don't know. It'll be a mystery forever, I suppose.

After talking to my father on the phone and convincing you and the doctor and the camp director that I hadn't intentionally taken any drugs, I slept at the infirmary for the night. In the morning, I returned to Gonzo cabin (the name becoming all too fitting, I'm sure, in your eyes) and everyone was really nice to me. I apologized for scaring everybody, for having you all out searching for me with flashlights after bedtime, but the incident was soon forgotten. I was fine.

Better than fine even. The second half of that summer was terrific. I got a new girlfriend, most importantly. Her name was Michelle. (A different Michelle, not the jokey Jon's sister. My girlfriend Michelle was in a different cabin from the girls I was friends with. As a further aside, writing this apology makes it clear that American parents should have chosen from a larger pool of names in the early 1970s.) Once again, you'd introduced me to her. Apparently, she had come to you expressing interest in me. I don't know why. Once again, she was a year older than me. And she was tall and very pretty, with big round eyes and curly auburn hair that shone blonde in the sun. Her teeth were straight and perfect; she'd gotten her braces off that year.

I had this yellow Brine Lacrosse T-shirt that I wore a lot that summer. It was emblazoned with the hilarious double entendre "Chicks with Sticks." (Looking back, this was surely a girls' lacrosse shirt. A fact that doesn't bother me at all now, but one I imagine might have when I was fourteen.

Either way, it was such poseur garb. I've never played lacrosse in my life.) But I was wearing it one day as Michelle and I were walking down the steps from the dining hall, holding hands, and a lady counselor I didn't even know stopped us and said, "You two are a really cute couple." That shirt became my favorite shirt after that.

And again, like the summer before, once I had secured a girlfriend, much of the ensuing time was spent looking for places where we could make out. Michelle and I found a suitably well-hidden tree house near the arts and crafts workshop. Immediately after dinner, the tennis courts were always empty; we'd lie down right next to the net sometimes. But these were often stressful, not entirely comfortable sessions, with too much energy put toward keeping an eye out for counselors and too much attention paid to the Swatch on Michelle's wrist.

Our problems, and those of Fernando and Becca and Geoff and Stephanie and the rest of us, were solved when the counselor of the girls' cabin disappeared for a week. As seems more than obvious in looking back, as was apparent to us even then, this counselor was having some problems in her life. She was a large woman, deeply hippied out, always a burst of color in flowing patchwork robes and flowers and beads and head wraps and stuff, but also gruff and unfriendly. I remember her chanting and dancing around the bonfire one night in a way that tipped past groovy fun and into occult ceremony in its intensity. Her eyes were rolling back in her head; I was waiting for her to pull out a rooster and slit its throat. (There were a lot of Wiccans up in that area of Maine, I learned from the other Gonzo cabin counselor, Eric, who was like the tie-dye master at the camp and whose family were Wiccans, or "witches," as he frankly put it when we were talking about Stevie Nicks one day. "I come from a family of witches," he said. He said some of them even believed in magic potions and spells and stuff, though he didn't so much himself. I don't mean to impugn Wicca in general here, of course. It actually seems like a pretty nice religion, as far as religions go. But that lady definitely scared some children. Me, a little, for one.)

A few days later, the girls told us that she had stayed out all night and returned to the cabin in the morning, after they'd woken up. She was the only counselor in their cabin at that point—another one had left after getting sick or something. She was in a bad mood, they said, and had told the girls not to tell any of the other counselors. They didn't like her very much, and it seemed pretty clear that she didn't like them, either, but she offered them a conspiratorial deal: "I don't want to be here; I know you don't want me here; keep your mouths shut and you get to sleep, or not sleep, in an unsupervised cabin." She knew they'd go for it. What group of teenagers wouldn't? But she also didn't seem to care a lot. I don't think she liked her job.

We boys didn't say anything, either. We wanted to tell you, if only just to talk to you about it, to get the gossip on this woman: Did you know what was up with her? Was this the craziest thing you'd ever heard? But when it happened again, the next day, when the girls told us that it did in fact appear that they had been left counselorless for the foreseeable future, we realized this was a situation to exploit.

We made a plan. We wore jeans and T-shirts into bed that night and set our digital watches to beep at midnight, after you and Eric would be asleep. I didn't even need the alarm. A mischievous thrill kept me awake until it was time, when I climbed down off my bunk and met the other guys in the dark. Without a word, we crept past your bed to the cabin's door. I held my breath as I pulled it open—slowly, slowly, cringing at the squeak of the hinges—and holding the handle for a second longer than I had to once it had closed. Then after waiting for a moment to make sure we were clear—half expecting to see a light go on, to hear your voice—the rush of the cool Maine air struck us as we snuck off over the soft pad of pine needles.

When we got to the girls' cabin, we whispered our amazement that this was happening. It was a dream come true: our own clubhouse, free of adult authority, at just the time in our lives when this was becoming the most exciting prospect imaginable. We could stay up all night. The girls had hung tapestries over the windows, and we had a couple of flashlights for light. We could do whatever we wanted. We played truth or dare, of course. (Wendy on the explicit condition that she never be made to kiss me; I didn't care.) And we went on spooky moonlit sorties around the camp, which we learned was crawling in the wee hours with skunks, which we gave wide berth, so as not to get sprayed and which I told

Christina were called *fish* in English, so that she would point and exclaim, "Look…look! The *feesh*! The *feesh*!" in her shy Castilian accent. And we all had a good laugh at that. So I owe her an apology, too, I guess, for such an obnoxious and xenophobic joke. Even though we fessed up and let her in on it soon enough. And she laughed along, blushing but unhurt. Knowing it was all in young, dumb fun.

My Michelle wasn't there that first time. But I told her about it the next day—trusting her with the secret of why we were all so baggy eyed but euphoric—and when we did it again the next night, I met her outside her cabin and brought her along. So when Fernando tucked himself into Becca's bed and Geoff into Stephanie's, Michelle and I spread out a sleeping bag on the floor and spent most of the night that way. And the night after that. Michelle was less adventurous than Wendy had been the summer before. (It became apparent early on in our kissing sessions that my packs of condoms would remain very much unopened.) Still, I wasn't complaining. I couldn't believe my luck.

Then we got caught. I forget how exactly we got caught, strangely. My memory must be hazier for the sleeplessness. I don't think we were found in flagrante. And I don't think we ever woke you as we slipped back in at dawn. Had someone ratted us out? Had a counselor from another cabin busted the girls? Had Jay grilled them and someone cracked? However it got back to you, you came into the cabin one afternoon with your nostrils flaring and ordered Geoff, Fernando, Jon, and me outside to the picnic table under the pine trees.

"You burned me," you said, shaking your head like you couldn't believe it.

You were mad in a way that I hadn't seen you before. I'd seen you spaz out at other adults, at refs, arguing calls during camp soccer games; I'd seen spittle fly out the corners of your mouth while you shouted from the sidelines wide-eyed with rage. This was different. You were honestly, earnestly angry in a different, more serious way. And embarrassed. It could not have been good news to get from another counselor, or worse, from Jay, your boss. I'm sure you had been called to account yourself. But beyond that, you were hurt. You looked at me with a hurt in your eyes. A look that confirmed to me that you did indeed consider us friends, outside of the fact that you were my counselor at camp. Or that you *had*, at least. Because the look in your eyes also conveyed the idea that something had changed between us. You had realized a sad truth, one that I was semiconscious of myself. That there was something in the way of our being friends as friends, something blocking us from a pure friendship that transcended the fact that you were my counselor at camp. It was just that: the official component of our relationship, the fact that you *were* my counselor at camp. I had betrayed you, I had burned you, I had been unable not to burn you—no matter how kind you'd been to me, no matter how much you'd helped me, no matter how many girlfriends you had set me up with, no matter how much I liked you as a person even—simply because you were technically an authority figure. I had to burn you. Surely, to a certain extent, you knew this. Surely, in the back of your mind, you must have expected it. You who had taught me so much about '60s rock.

"I can't even talk to you right now," you said.

And you didn't talk to us, or to me at least, for days after that. Days that felt turgid and overripe with uncomfortable cohabitation and much less laughter in Gonzo cabin than there had been before—and I knew that it was I who had spoiled things. But you are a good person, and those long-stretching days let feelings heal, and during the last week of camp, you gave me the great honor of letting me lead my own session of the '60s Rock elective.

That afternoon, once the group had assembled, you gave me a nice, flattering introduction—noting that I was the first camper ever to assume such a role in the elective that you had created. I had taken the task seriously and devoted the day to the Rolling Stones, who had replaced Led Zeppelin as my all-time favorite band that year, and made a syllabus of songs to play and discuss. I brought a bunch of tapes—*Let It Bleed*, *Sticky Fingers*, *Get Yer Ya-Ya's Out!*—and the *Encyclopedia of Rock* book that I had brought with me to camp, and the big history of the Stones book with the red cover, and the one with the cover from *Black and Blue*, and we looked up release dates and liner notes credits. I remember we came to the conclusion that, as much as I wished it were otherwise, Keith Richards, who was my favorite Rolling Stone and personal rock hero, did not play the guitar solo on the live version of "Sympathy for the Devil" from *Get Yer Ya-Ya's Out!* It must have been Mick Taylor.

But I was sure to credit Keith with what, for me at that point, might have been his most important contribution to the band and to rock 'n' roll in general and what it all meant to me. In between song selections, I told the story of the famous drug bust at the Redlands estate in 1967, and how when the prosecutor brought up the fact that Marianne Faithfull had been found wearing nothing but a bearskin rug, Keith had replied, in front of a packed courtroom, "We are not old men. We are not worried about petty morals."

I still get a thrill from that quote, to tell you the truth. I still like the ideas it embodies. (Even as I approach the wrong side of the equation myself.) But looking back at that summer and at the way I put some of those ideas into action, I'm sorry to have put you on the other side of the equation, sorry to have let you down the way that I did. There were things I didn't yet understand about friendship, and about trust and gratitude and respect. Things that I should have appreciated but did not.

HIGH SCHOOL

(Or when being drunk becomes the excuse for everything, even though it is never a legitimate excuse for anything.)

Dear BMX Bike Rider,

I'm sorry for shunning you after you got up in front of everyone and cried at the personal growth workshop our parents sent us to in Philadelphia.

We were around the same age, fifteen. I had recently started getting into trouble at home, caught drinking for the first time and lying to my parents. They were psychologists, my parents, former hippies from the '60s. ("Flower children" has always been my mom's preferred term.) They were pretty permissive as disciplinarians and understanding in terms of expectations. My dad used to tell me, "Every generation of teenagers thinks they're discovering sex, drugs, and rock 'n' roll for the first time. And no one ever is."

But in the '80s, they were into a lot of this New Agey personal-development stuff. I don't think they ever did EST per se, but they were in a group called Marriage Encounter that was based on the same ideas, and they'd been going to these Insight Transformational Seminars. It was cool for them; they felt like they got a lot out of it. But it was really very definitively not my thing. So when, in lieu of a harsher punishment and in the expressed hope that it would help us communicate better as a family, they signed me up for the youth version, Teen Insight, and insisted I attend, it was one of the times I considered running away from home.

I imagine you can relate. You did back then. You were a skate rat. And, you said, a professionally sponsored BMX "freestyle" rider. You'd brought your bike with you, in fact, and impressed everyone with what were certainly professional-looking stunts—bunny hopping down steps, doing a handstand off the seat while balancing on one wheel, that sort of thing. You wore your bangs hanging down over your eyes, and a wiseass sneer, and some very punk rock shredder gear that I realized was infinitely cooler than the Brine Lacrosse "Chicks with Sticks" T-shirt that I was wearing.

It was called the Awakening Heart Seminar for god's sake. (I can still taste the puke in my mouth.) But there we were, Friday night, sitting on the floor in the beige conference room of some corporate park hotel outside Philadelphia, where we were encouraged by a man and a woman with voices like easy-listening radio DJs to take part in first-day-of-camp get-to-know-you exercises with thirty or so other teenagers we'd never met before. There were hand-drawn posters and signs on the walls, daily affirmation–type slogans written in thick colored marker. "If it takes all night, that'll be all right. If I can get you to smile before I leave." Fucking Jackson Browne.

I was very surprised to see how receptive many of the other kids were. Some had done the seminar before, I learned, or ones like it. Many of them, apparently, were there not under duress but of their own volition. And an astounding number of them leaped right in with the sharing and the singing and the hugging and expressing. It didn't take long at all to get them to smile.

We were smiling, too, after a while. And laughing. You and me and a small group of what I considered to be normal teenagers had taken to making jokes at the ridiculousness of all of this—often at the expense of the leaders and those so willing to participate. I remember the faces but none of the names. There was the lanky guy with the fake front tooth that he could flip in and out with his tongue, who wore a denim jacket with the cover to the Smiths' *Meat Is Murder* album painted on the back. The black guy, who I think was the only black person there, with the peach-fuzz mustache. And two girls, a shorter one with curly dark hair and a taller one with glasses. The tall girl was sour and sexy like Catherine Keener, and I'm sure we all fell in love with her immediately. I did anyway. We sat at the far edge of the assembly, this crew, and cracked ourselves up in an enjoyably mean-spirited way. Under our breath, of course. But it was surely obvious to everybody what was going on. We didn't make much of an effort to hide our disdain.

It was a horrible sort of prison. The hours passed as slowly as hours can. There was great pressure to participate, to open up and share our feelings. But the six of us supported each other in holding out. At one point, I was surrounded by a crowd of the other kids, the ones with awakened hearts, who were urging me to take part in one of the exercises—talk about my fears, my innermost wishes, or make a list of words to describe my parents. Someone literally asked me, "Why are you hiding inside this shell?" It was a difficult moment. They'd backed me into a corner, like in a zombie movie. I looked out over their heads, frantic, searching for help. When I spotted you and the Smiths jacket guy standing off to the side, snickering and making eyes at me like, "Ha-ha—better you than me," it was exactly the type of sympathy I needed to get through. Thanks.

The leaders had asked that we not use drugs or alcohol for the duration of the seminar as that could interfere with the sensitive personal growth and development processes that were supposed to be taking place. So of course, during Saturday's lunch break, we got a ride into West Philadelphia with an older kid with a driver's license and his parents' BMW to buy a bag of pot and a case of beer and had a really fun party that night in one of the girls' rooms in the hotel. It *was* like camp it turned out, even for those of us who didn't go along with the official program, in that we got very close very quickly.

We were all bleary come Sunday. Goofy and even more obnoxious for our lack of sleep. Maybe that's why things got weird. We were back in the conference room, sitting on the floor in our spot in the back, cracking jokes while people took turns standing at a podium, talking about what they'd learned about themselves so far. It was an extremely emotional scene by that point; there was a huge amount of hugging and holding hands and stroking of hair and stuff—among the others, I mean.

I can understand how it could happen, a fifteen-year-old kid, hungover, in that strangely charged atmosphere—but still, it came as a major shock to suddenly see you up on the stage at the front of the room. You'd been sitting right next to me. I hadn't even noticed you getting up.

You started hesitantly, mumbling words and hiding behind your bangs. But then your shoulders fell and you let out a loud sob, and then you were bawling and shaking, talking about how much you loved your dad but you couldn't tell him, about how you felt judged. You cried and talked for a long time. The leaders hugged you when you stepped down. A lot of people hugged you. Regardless of how cultish and after-school special it all was, I think this was maybe a good thing for you.

Needless to say, it was uncomfortable for all of us when you came back to where we were sitting. You looked at us apologetically—you knew the rules. One of the girls put her hand on your shoulder. But none of us said anything, and the other guys were like me in avoiding eye contact with you.

You didn't sit with us for long. There was some other activity soon, and for the rest of the day, you joined the others, the participators, in more hugging and crying and stroking hair and talking about feelings. As soon as you were out of earshot, we talked about how weird it was, how we had lost you, and so abruptly with no warning. We made fun of you, as I'm sure you were aware. But I doubt that bothered you.

You didn't look sad. You looked relieved. In fact, you were beaming.

■ ■ ■

Dear Judy Gailhouse,

Sorry for letting your children watch *The Amityville Horror*.

This was at the house on Long Beach Island that you and your husband, Michael, and my parents and a bunch of your other friends rented every summer. I shouldn't even have been there. I didn't want to be there. I was not supposed to be there. I was supposed to be at home, at my parents' house, where I had been given the responsibility of staying by myself for the week.

Of course, I had a party on the very first night. I'd had unsupervised parties before—over winter weekends during the school year, when my parents were away skiing—and been able to clean up well enough before they returned to avoid getting caught. But this was in the summer, and the party got bigger and more out of control than the others had. A door got broken; Kool-Aid was made with beer on the kitchen floor; a metal fork was microwaved, causing a flash of light and a booming explosion that knocked the microwave off the counter onto the Kool-Aid-covered floor. (Amazingly, it still worked when I set it back up and plugged it back in. But

I've wondered for years whether or not this might have had anything to do with the fact that both my parents got cancer later. Probably not. We lived in New Jersey; chances are they both would have gotten cancer anyway.) Bottles broke in the pool. Peanut butter somehow ended up all over the living room curtains. No one died, that was lucky. But after spending a sad, hungover next day trying to make repairs and hide evidence, I realized that I was going to have to fess up this time. I called my parents, who were understandably unhappy to hear the news, and my dad drove home to pick me up and bring me down to Long Beach Island, where I was to not leave the house for the rest of the week.

That hour-long car ride was no fun at all. My dad was about as mad as I'd ever made him. But he wasn't yelling or scolding me. He was not looking at me. He was disgusted. I tried to muster up some disaffected indignation in return, but I couldn't pull it off. He was right to be angry. I would have liked to be able to say, "God, what's the big deal?" But I knew what was the big deal.

We drove in silence. South down the Garden State Parkway on a sunny Monday in summer. The trees got pinier the farther we got; the grass at the side of the road turned to sand. After a long while, my father spoke. He told me he understood about thinking that I was old enough to handle things that I couldn't handle and thinking I knew everything even when I didn't. He said it hurt him that he couldn't trust me anymore, but that he even understood that. He understood rebellion. But he said that I was still his son, still living in his house. And if I was going to make his life less pleasant, he would make my life less pleasant. "You got your job and I got mine," he said.

There was an acknowledgment in the phrase that felt honest, that I appreciated. But it also felt a little bit like good-bye.

The rest of the week was an effective punishment. Anywhere my family was was absolutely the last place I wanted to be at that point in my life. The other kids that were there—your children, my sister, and four or five others—were all at least five years younger than me. My parents were mad at me, but of course, you guys and the other adults weren't. You gave me some good-natured teasing upon my arrival.

"Why weren't we invited?" you asked with a smile.

I grumbled something surly, too embarrassed to take anything good-naturedly.

To add insult to injury, I learned that some of you were going up to the roof deck to smoke pot after dinner every night—which had the devastating effect of making me feel jealous of, and less cool than, my parents' forty-five-year-old friends. I spent most of the week alone in a room reading magazines and listening to LL Cool J's *Radio* album. But not even on a big woofer box that I could have played at volumes intended to offend older ears. Just on my Walkman.

One night I was in the TV room, flipping channels to find something to watch, when Sarah Landy and my sister and your two boys, Patrick and Eddie, came in. Sarah was ten or eleven. Patrick must have been eight or so, my sister seven,

Eddie five. There was only one TV in the house, so I stayed sitting there and tried to pretend they didn't exist. It turned out *The Amityville Horror* was on. I stopped flipping, at least partially in hopes that it might chase them out of the room. I warned them that it was a scary movie. But they stayed and I absolved myself from any responsibility. I wasn't there to babysit. I was trying to mope.

The kids became transfixed, as kids will do in front of a television, and it was quiet, which I liked. After about half an hour—after the buzzing of the flies, after the statue falling on the priest in the church, after James Brolin sees his face in the fire—little Eddie burst out wailing like an ambulance siren. He was inconsolable, totally freaking out. Sarah got up and led him downstairs.

I knew I'd fucked up, and it occurred to me that I might be hearing more about it, but I was determined to play out what I saw as my role as the blasé no-goodnik. So when you came up to fetch Patrick and my sister, and looked at the screen, and then at me, and said, "Real nice, Dave. Thanks a lot," I gave you a well-rehearsed "whatever" shrug and turned back to the TV.

So you have my sympathy, as well as an apology. I know I wouldn't like it if some sullen teenager showed up in the middle of my nice beach vacation and showed my kid that movie. If it's any consolation, I didn't sleep well at all that night. I kept seeing James Brolin seeing his face in that fire. That shit is terrifying.

■ ■ ■

Dear Mr. McCormack,

I'm sorry for rejoicing over the prospect of your hometown being destroyed.

I should never have been in the French 2 class you were teaching in the first place. The teacher who had taught the French 1 class I had taken the previous year had been a sadsack pushover and either didn't notice or didn't care that I had been cheating on pretty much every test he gave, and so awarded me a passing grade even though I hadn't learned how to say much more than "*Je m'appelle David.*" Oh, and the words for "to dance" and "to sing," *danser* and *chanter*—for some reason those always stuck in my head.

So that very first day, when you greeted the class in French (and with such a perfect accent—you were actually *from* France, I was surprised to learn!) and kept talking to us that way, like we were supposed to understand what you were saying, well, I had a pretty good idea that I wasn't going to be able to bluff my way through for very long. It being the start of a new school year, we students were rambunctious— laughing, joking, still half-fried from summer. You asserted your authority. Standing at the front of the class, not smiling, you spoke to us sternly, all these crisp, mellifluous words I didn't understand. Eventually I was made to know that you expected us all to write a one-page essay about what we did over the summer, *in French*. You handed out paper. I looked around. Were you serious? There was no way I could do anything like that. Could anyone else? Just how far behind had all that cheating left me? Quite far apparently as most of the class set themselves to writing. You sat down at your desk.

I stared at the empty page, marveling at how hopeless my situation was, thinking about the old saying about how when you cheat, you're really only cheating yourself. Well, here I was. I decided to give it my best shot.

Je m'appelle David, I started. *Mon vacacion de summer c'was magnifique...*

I wrote more like this, sprinkling the few French words I knew among the mostly English bullshit. *Le weather was tres bien.* I wrote the letters as big as I could, gave myself two-inch margins, took up as much space as possible with cross-outs. Still, I looked at the page: a quarter full; it was ridiculous. So I decided to make it more ridiculous. I stood up and walked up to your desk. "Excuse me, Mr. McCormack?"

You corrected me. "*Excusez-moi—*"

"*Excusez-moi*, Monsieur McCormack. Where are you from in France? What city did you grow up in?"

"*D'où venez-vous...*"

"*D'où venez-vous...*"

"*Je suis Niçois*," you said with a quizzical expression. "*Je suis originaire de Nice.*"

"*Merci*," I said. I knew Nice was the name of a city in France. I even knew it was spelled like *nice*. I went back to my seat, sat down, and started writing again.

Mon favorite du jour de la summer, I wrote, *was when le president de Etas Unis, monsieur Ronald Reagan, declared war on La France. La jour de tres joueoux! When President Reagan dropped le bombs on le cite de Nice, all le garcons y all la femmes dances y chantes!*

Terribly obnoxious. And about half as clever as I thought it was. (Although considering it now, I wonder whether President Reagan ever did harbor a secret desire to attack France—and whether he ever did make an announcement like that, just as a joke, while recording a sound check for a radio address.) I cringe a little at the thought of what my face must have looked like as I passed my essay in, what yours must have looked like when you read it. The next morning during homeroom, I was called down to the principal's office where I was told that you did not want me to come to class anymore and that my mother had been called in for a meeting with you and me and the school's principal, Dr. Nogueira.

My mother was not happy to come to such a meeting, of course. And you and Dr. Nogueira were both frowning when we all sat down. I avoided eye contact with everyone and tried to suppress the smirk that so often crept onto my face when I was being reprimanded—a nervous reaction that was rarely taken for what it was. That day, though, I admit to feeling a bit of pride when you told my mother that you'd never been so personally offended in your career. My mother, who was a teacher herself, a professor at Rutgers, looked very sad. I was punished that night at dinner—a grounding.

My guidance counselor switched me out of French 2 and into Spanish 1. And I'm sure the next three years were better for it for all involved. You didn't hold a grudge. You were actually a very nice guy, one of the teachers at Red Bank Regional who seemed to honestly like and care about the kids. Seeing each other in the hallways, or on the class trips you sometimes chaperoned, we eventually developed a friendly rapport—in English, of course.

This year, as it turns out, I'm going to France for a vacation—five days in Paris, my first time there since I went with my dad when I was twelve. From what I've heard, it's still a place where speaking French comes in handy. So I will be at a disadvantage. Once again, I'll be reminded that it was only myself I was cheating all those years ago. I fully expect some waiter at a café will insult me to my face without my ever knowing. Hard to say I won't deserve it.

■ ■ ■

Dear Bob and Paula Cohen,

Sorry for the way I was dressed at Rick's bar mitzvah.

Our families were in a *havurah* group together. There were not so many Jews in the part of New Jersey where we lived, so you and my parents and the Rosens and the Feldmans and the Gainsburgs started a club that would gather on one Friday night a month and on holidays to say prayers and share a meal and talk about being Jewish. *Havurah* means "fellowship" in Hebrew.

The gatherings had grown less frequent by the time your son Rick, who'd recently dropped a *y* off the name we were to call him, turned thirteen, and stepped up on the bimah at Temple Beth Torah. The older kids in the group—Adam and Ariel, the Feldman girls, your daughter Lori and I—were all in high school and increasingly uninterested in spending Friday nights in the vicinity of our families. But attendance at bar and bat mitzvahs was still pretty much mandatory.

There was no way I was going to wear a coat and tie, though. I had developed a strong sense of fashion over the past year, having noticed that wearing the same types of shirts and shoes as the popular upperclassmen in my school would draw compliments from the girls in my grade. My style was hyper-preppy, accented with what I liked to think of as a sort of new-wave flare. Two polo shirts at a time, both collars turned up. Prefaded jeans with Jackson Pollock–style bleach splatters, carefully spaced so as to look haphazardly punk rock. (I can still smell the fumes rising from my bathtub, staying on my hands for days afterward.) L.L.Bean duck boots, laces left loose, but just so, with little knots tied at the ends to keep them from slipping out of place. Army Navy Store trench coat and as much Ralph Lauren as I could convince my parents to buy me—something that I did most successfully by telling them that wearing nice clothes made me feel better about myself. All of this is embarrassing to remember.

My father hated it. He was not particularly frugal (bucking

stereotype!). But clothes were the last thing he would have chosen to spend money on. The fact that he did so for me gave me a glimpse into a truth about parenthood that I couldn't fully understand at the time.

One day around this time, I walked into his office with a mind to start a philosophical argument. "Everything that anybody ever does is selfish," I said.

"What do you mean?" he said, turning in his chair. This was the type of discussion he liked.

"Well." I had been thinking about it for a while. "People control their own actions. We choose what we do. And even when we do something nice for someone else, we get something in return. We're rewarded for doing the nice thing. And that's why we do it."

"Hmm." My father's eyes narrowed.

"Even if the reward is just a thank-you. That makes us feel better about ourselves, so that's why we do it. Even if the person you help doesn't say thank you, you still get a reward. Even if it's just a smile. Or even if it's not a smile. Even if it's nothing you can see. Just knowing you helped someone can be the reward. It feels good to help someone. When I do something nice for someone, something that makes someone else happy, or feel better or something, that makes *me* happy. It makes me feel better about *myself.* I know this and that's why I ever do anything nice for someone. To make myself feel good. I choose to do it, to get something, this good feeling, for myself. So it's really totally selfish in the end."

He considered it for a minute and then disagreed. "No, I

can think of times where I do something totally for someone else," he said. "For you. And your sister. There are times where I do things for you not because it makes me happy to do it, but just because it makes you happy."

"But making me happy makes you happy," I said. "Otherwise you wouldn't do it."

"No, there's a difference. And I don't expect you to necessarily be able to understand it. But there are times when I do something that I really don't want to do, just because it makes you happy. But not because it makes me happy to see you happy. It's something else."

"But I mean, you choose to do it. At some level it must be making you happy."

"I don't think so," he said and paused a moment. "Like with your clothes. I don't want to spend all this crazy money on clothes. You know that. I think it's gross. And it doesn't make me happy to see you happy about something like expensive clothes. If anything, it makes me sad. I feel kinda guilty about it actually. I'm not sure it's the right thing to do; I'm not sure I think it's good for you. But your mom and I talked about it, and we do it anyway. We do it because of the time you told me that wearing these clothes makes you feel better about yourself. It's hard to explain. It has to do with being a parent."

I didn't like this answer at all. I didn't like him making a claim to some mysterious secret knowledge that I didn't have access to. (He was right, though. And now that I have my own kid, I better understand what he was getting at—the extent to which, as a parent, you're living more for another person than you are for yourself.)

Anyway, the day of Rick's bar mitzvah, I stepped into the synagogue wearing a Polo oxford shirt, untucked, over a Polo polo shirt with the collar popped up, army fatigues pants that were short enough to show off the argyle socks I had on, and new penny loafers. I had also just gotten a haircut, shaved close on the sides, left longer on top, in the surfer style that was in vogue at the time. So I looked like a sort of mushroom-headed caricature of a villain from a John Hughes movie. Strangely, I liked this. The villains in John Hughes movies were always snobby jerks, but they always had superhot girlfriends. I imagined a song by Echo & the Bunnymen playing as I walked through the lobby.

People, all of them dressed more formally than I was, shot me looks as I passed. Or at least I imagined they did. I did not know a lot of people there—only those in our *havurah* group. After the ceremony in the reception hall, I sat at Lonnie's table with Adam and Ariel and one of the Feldman girls and a few other kids I didn't know. We complained about being forced to endure Kool & the Gang's "Celebration" at every single bar mitzvah any of us had ever been to and made jokes about the things we would say to Ernie Anastos, the anchorman for Channel 7 News, who was in attendance, apparently being an old friend of yours, if any of us worked up the gumption to approach him. ("Are you *theeeee* Ernie Anastos?" I suggested and laughed. Though that isn't funny at all.) None of us did, of course.

Rick and his seventh-grade classmates slid across the parquet dance floor in their socks, the boys throwing their yarmulkes like Frisbees, the girls taller than them and more self-controlled. The adults danced, including my parents, early and enthusiastically, horrifying me as they did at every bar or bat mitzvah or wedding we went to, with their jitterbug moves and big smiles on their faces. They were good dancers. Or just fine ones, at least. It's funny how every adolescent is so embarrassed by the sight of his or her parents dancing and thinks it's because the parents are such terrible, dorky dancers, when what is surely at the root of the embarrassment is the realization of how much more comfortable in their own bodies the parents are than the adolescents—how much more able to relax and let themselves have fun, how much freer from the paralyzing effects of self-consciousness.

I didn't get up from my seat for the whole party. What energy I expended went toward making sure that everyone around me knew how lame I thought everything was. I hoped that all the other guests there, all the younger kids, all the adults, would look over at me and see a teenager with a capital T. Radical, rebellious, possibly even dangerous.

In my argyle socks.

Obviously, I was very confused about a lot things.

■ ■ ■

Dear Girl from California,

I'm sorry I didn't try to kiss you.

You were visiting your friend Kristen Anderson. She'd moved to my town that year and had James Cash and me over to drink wine coolers at her house while her mom was out for the night. As you might remember, James and Kristen had gone into Kristen's room, leaving you and me out on the couch in the living room watching Cynthia Gibb and Rob Lowe in *Youngblood* on HBO.

I don't remember your name. But you were very pretty, and I certainly did want to kiss you.

In all honesty, I wanted to do much more than that. I don't know about you, but I was still a virgin at the time. A condition that had me ruing my decision, two summers prior, to bring a pack of condoms to camp in hopes of having sex with a girl named Wendy Siegler. Those hopes turned out to have been in vain. And those condoms—most of them collecting dust in a drawer in the desk in my room, one of them creating the all-too-clichéd ring in the leather of my wallet—had since turned into a heavy dead albatross around my neck. (Only metaphorically, of course.) I hadn't come anywhere close to needing a condom since then. And I couldn't escape the thought, as ridiculous as I knew it was, that I had jinxed myself. Those condoms sat in their wrappers mocking me, stretching each day that passed with them unopened into an eternity, giving me my first real sense of mortality, in fact: every night as I fell asleep at that time of my life, my last waking thought was a prayer to god to not let me die before I had sex.

Unfortunately, despite all this, and despite the fact that it was just you and me sitting alone in a room with no lights on in a house with no parents in it, despite however many wine coolers we'd drunk, I could not find the courage to unpin myself from the far corner of the couch and slide over next to you. Not even during that incredibly explicit sex scene when Cynthia Gibb comes to visit Rob Lowe in the boarding room with the wood-burning stove. We hadn't spoken for a while by the time that scene came on, and we didn't say anything while it was on. We just sat there watching naked Cynthia Gibb and Rob Lowe flop down on the mattress they'd thrown onto the floor, listening to their breathing and grunting and the sound of their sweat-slick bodies writhing around and atop each other.

I realized that this was precisely the type of opportunity teenage virgins were supposed to act on. (For what other reason is a movie like *Youngblood* made?) I knew I should be trying to kiss you. But I didn't know what to do. Make a joke to break the tension first? Say something suave and sexy and scoot myself over to your side of the couch? Get up, walk over there, sit back down, and just plant one on you?

You shifted in your seat, drawing your legs up under you, pulling them back out again—a sign surely, I thought. But of what, I didn't understand. You weren't glancing over at me as I was so often at you. It seemed like you might be bored. I felt like I was being concurrently blessed and punished by god. (The god I prayed to every night without really believing in.) I couldn't feel my legs.

Soon after the scene ended, you got up without a word and left me there sitting by myself. I felt like a giant loser. And guessed that I'd never had a shot with you anyway.

The following Monday, though, when I saw Kristen on the bus to school, she told me that you were mad at me. That you had indeed wanted to fool around with me, too, and that you were mad that I hadn't made a move. And that you'd already taken a plane back to California.

It's hard to describe how sorry I felt at that moment.

■ ■ ■

Dear Mrs. Martinez,

Sorry for having Jennifer McCartney call you and pretend to be my mom so I could cut school and go to the Sting concert at Madison Square Garden.

This was February 1988. You were the secretary at the Red Bank Regional principal's office. We had come to know each other quite well during my first few years of high school. I spent a lot of time in that office because I got in trouble a lot, and it was your job to schedule meetings for me with one of the vice principals, Mr. Moses or Mr. Conlin, or sometimes the head principal, Dr. Nogueira, and write up the forms assigning me to a punishment of Saturday morning detention or in-school suspension or, in a few extreme instances, full-fledged suspension. Saturday morning detention was sort of like the movie *The Breakfast Club*—except that at Red Bank Regional, the sessions were only two hours long and held in the cafeteria, not the library, and there were always like a hundred kids there instead of a perfect quintet representing the platonic ideals of white suburban teenager stereotypes. You had recently told me that I had broken the school record for Saturday morning detentions. I had been scheduled to be there every Saturday for the remainder of the year, a full book, and so was to be given in-school suspension upon all subsequent infractions.

As mind-numbingly boring as in-school suspension was (detainees were to sit silently in a single classroom and work on extra assignments sent by the teachers of the classes they were missing for the full six-hour school day), part of me was proud of my accomplishment. (A new record!) The same part of me that had been smirking a couple of months prior, when I had walked into your office one sunny Monday morning wearing handcuffs, chaperoned by a police officer. I had just gotten my driver's license; it was my first day driving myself to school, and my friend Matt was home on Christmas break from the boarding school he went to in Rhode Island. We rarely got a chance to see each other, Matt and I, so we'd made a plan that involved him stealing beer from his parents' garage, and me picking him up, and us going to park somewhere and get drunk. Things went very wrong with the last part obviously. (We chose a bad place to park.) And after we'd spent an hour behind bars, occupying the only two jail cells in the Little Silver police station, singing "Nobody Knows the Trouble I've Seen," like you're supposed to if you were raised on Bugs Bunny cartoons, after Matt's very angry mother had come to fetch him, the arresting officer had brought me to the school, because since I was still a minor, I was the administration's legal responsibility during school hours. This is a policy that rewards illegal teenage activity. As there is nothing that makes you feel cooler, more like Keith Richards, than being paraded down your crowded high school hallway, half-drunk, wearing handcuffs, in the custody of a uniformed police officer. That was one of the incidents that earned me a full-fledged suspension—another ill-thought "punishment": not being in school being far preferable to being in school. (This aspect was, however, counterbalanced by the fact that I lost my driver's license for six months and had to go to these classes about the dangers of drinking and driving.) When you saw me that day, you just shook your head, and when you told me that I had broken the school record for Saturday morning detentions, you didn't say it like "Congratulations!" I think we had different senses of humor, you and I.

Well, the day of the Sting concert—to which Liz Dilascia had gotten tickets for herself and Kate Hendrickx and Melody Moses and me—we had decided to leave school early. We planned to cut the last three or four class periods, in order to take an early enough train into New York to fully exploit the unlimited-pitchers-of-beer deal that the Beefsteak Charlie's outside Madison Square Garden offered with a steak dinner. We had fake IDs.

Liz and Kate and Melody had lined up their excuses, or they were just planning to take the Saturday detention that came with skipping classes. I couldn't afford that; unsanctioned absence would land me an in-school detention. And further trouble at home. I'd only recently gotten off grounding. I needed permission.

Melody came up with the idea of calling the office from one of the pay phones in the commons. We could pretend it was my mom calling and say that I had a doctor's appointment or a funeral to go to. But Melody was giggly by nature and didn't trust herself not to crack up. Our friend Jennifer, tougher and always ready to tempt trouble, volunteered.

The commons was a spacious, echoey, brick-walled area that was, as you know, loudly filled with students between periods. Jen had to make the call when it was quieter, so she asked to go to the bathroom in the middle of a class before lunch, quarters in her purse. We weren't worried that you'd somehow know the call was coming from within the building, that there was some kind of light-button alert or phone-tap system, because the year before a guy from the class above ours had gotten the entire school a two-hour reprieve from our drudgery by calling in a bomb threat from those very phones. He'd chosen a nice spring day for his stunt, so we all got to hang out in the parking lot, sitting on car hoods or playing hacky sack while the fire department brought in bomb-sniffing dogs and everything. It was very exciting! I couldn't believe it worked, and I wondered why someone braver than I was didn't make such a phone call each and every day. (I can see now why such a thing is not good to do.)

Jen's call was not as successful. As she told me later, when we met in the hallway, "Sorry. You're totally busted."

"Fuck," I said.

"I tried my best," Jen said. She felt bad. But mostly, we were laughing. "I thought I did a good job. I told her you had a doctor's appointment, but that I was at Rutgers—I even put the details in there—so I couldn't come in to sign you out in person."

"How'd she know?" I asked. "What did she say?"

"She didn't buy it for a second. She said, 'I don't know who this is, but I know it's not Brenna Bry.' I remained calm. I said I had a cold. She didn't believe me. She said, 'I talk to Dr. Bry on the phone at least once a week, and this doesn't sound anything like her. And I'm going to talk to her again today, as soon as I get off the phone with you, whichever one of David's friends this is.' She told me to tell you that."

"What!?" This was upsetting. I had no idea you talked to my mom so often. What did you talk to her about? (Me obviously. I learned later that my mother had taken to calling in to get weekly attendance reports.)

"I didn't know what to say," Jen went on. "I tried to sound insulted and act mad and stuff, but it wasn't working. So I hung up. And I guess she's gonna call your mom? I'm sorry."

I left school early anyway and took the train into Penn Station and went to Beefsteak Charlie's and the concert. Liz,

Kate, and Melody were three pretty, popular girls, and there was no way I was going to break a date with them—even at the prospect, even at the guarantee, of in-school suspension and parental punishment. "I don't care," I said. "They can't tell me what to do."

Mostly, this speaks to just how misguided and, in fact, deeply conformist all my efforts at rebelling truly were. The notion of losing face, of seeming less than fearless and care-free in front of my friends, was scarier than any threat you or the school or my parents could hold over me. It was the worst thing I could imagine.

Of course, the fact that I was as psyched as I was to go to a Sting concert doesn't speak so well for my thinking at the time, either. As great as the Police were—and they were very, very great. I had all their records and multiple posters of them on the walls of my bedroom. One of their lyric passages in particular, from "Born in the '50s," a song on their first album, had resonated with me throughout my teenage years: "You don't understand us/So don't reprimand us/We're taking the future/We don't need no teacher!" I took that as a sort of mission statement; I remember writing it on the cover of my science notebook freshman year.

By 1988, though, Sting had started the descent that would reach its nadir twelve years later with the infamous television commercial that featured him standing onstage, in front of an audience, and closing his eyes as the scene flashed to him sitting in the backseat of a chauffeured Jaguar sedan and words appeared on the screen that said, "What then do rock stars dream of?" Do you remember that one? I try to be as for-giving a person as I can be. People deserve a little slack—here I am, asking your forgiveness right now. But this, Sting's Jaguar commercial, which tells us that while his fans, peo-ple who have presumably paid money to come see him, are watching him perform and thinking about him and his mu-sic, he is thinking about being driven around in his extremely expensive luxury car, this I will never be able to forgive. By 1988, Sting was singing smooth jazz-fusion world-music songs about the widows of Chilean political dissidents—way, way too earnestly. And taking himself way, way, way too se-riously. The concert I skipped out of school to see was in support of an album that took its title from a Shakespearean sonnet. He'd recently remade the Police classic "Don't Stand So Close to Me" (which, to dock credit where it's due to be docked, already cited Nabokov, and clumsily) into a humor-less, soft-synth, elevator shell of its former self. But when he performed it at MSG that night, bathed in spotlight, arms outstretched like Jesus, wearing some sort of long white robe shirt, like an Indian kurta pajama thing, I was enrapt, clutch-ing my hands to my chest, singing along to every word. Oy. It makes me want to puke up all the beer you can drink.

Afterward, after the blurry train trip back to Little Silver and the unsafe ride home from one of the girls, I opened the door to my house expecting my parents to be standing there, enraged. But I don't even think they had waited up. They'd left a note. "Hope you enjoyed the concert. You're grounded again." You had indeed called my mom. It was to be another two weeks before I was allowed to leave the house for any reason other than to go to school. But there was no yelling or screaming or slamming of palms on the dinner table. They were quietly disappointed and didn't know what to do. It must have been very frustrating. They were tired of me.

Soon, though, after the grounding ended, they sat me down at that table for a talk. (Or they sat down. I leaned against the kitchen island sink.) "You're seventeen years old," my dad said flatly. "That's too old for us to be punishing you. Too old for us to control. So for the next year and a half, while you still have to live in this house, we're not going to punish you anymore."

"We know that you're drinking and using drugs," my mom said. "And we don't approve. But it's more important to us that you stay safe and that you tell us the truth."

"We're not saying that we like it," my dad said. "We're not giving you permission to do whatever you want. But we won't be punishing you anymore. On one condition: No more lying. No more sneaking around. You tell us the truth, no more grounding from here on out."

I was stunned. And stayed silent for a moment before leaping to accept the deal. No more punishing. No more parental authority. I had made it. I was free.

It was something I had been wanting for five years. Taking the future, not needing no teacher. And even though I would keep fucking things up for myself for a good while longer, sort of stumbling into my new, teacherless future, I did stop listening to Sting's solo records soon thereafter—and I look back at the episode as the best thing that ever happened in terms of the relationship between me and my parents. So thank you, for the part you played.

And sorry for insulting your intelligence.

■ ■ ■

Dear Sean Something,

Sorry for having sex with your girlfriend.

It was really not like me to do something like that, to have sex with someone else's girlfriend. In fact, up until that very moment—on a Friday night in May 1988—it was not like me to have sex with anyone. By which I mean to say that your girlfriend was the first person I ever had sex with.

A couple of weeks before school ended my junior year, two days after the prom, it was Senior Skip Day, when Red Bank Regional seniors were unofficially excused for cutting their classes and everyone usually went to the beach. WNEW was hosting their annual beach party to kick off Memorial Day weekend at the boardwalk in Asbury Park. Joan Jett and the Blackhearts were playing and George Thorogood and the Destroyers and the Georgia Satellites, who just the previous year had enjoyed their big MTV hit "Keep Your Hands to Yourself." So lots of us besides the seniors cut school to go. And lots of other kids from other schools, too, apparently. We'd all left the house at the normal time and gone to a gas station or 7-Eleven to get beer and load up coolers with ice instead of going to school. So by nine o'clock in the morning, the beach out in front of the old Casino on the pier, where they had set up a stage and the broadcast equipment, was filled with drunk teenagers. And some adults, too.

It was a perfect day. Sun shining down from a bright blue sky, a breeze blowing in off the ocean. Everyone all smiles and fives and cheers-ing strangers. Propeller planes flew up and down the shore trailing advertising banners; some of them advertising the radio station and the concert itself; some of them shaped like giant beer cans: Budweiser! Coors Light Silver Bullet! We held up our matching cans as they passed and said, "*Whooooo!*" We knew they were directed just at us; sometimes you could see the pilots waving. We all felt so lucky to be where we were: at a giant rock 'n' roll party on the beach instead of school. In heaven.

That day glows in my memory like no other. For one big resultant reason obviously. But that reason, the fact that I got to have sex for the first time, seems like the result of the glowing. Something was going on that day. I'm still not exactly sure what. But somehow, for some reason, out of however many thousands of us were out there feeling lucky to be on the beach that day, I'm pretty sure I was the single luckiest one of all. I made out with five girls that day. Five girls! I know this type of tallying looks silly in twenty-four years' hindsight. (And that to some people, Wilt Chamberlain, say, the tally itself wouldn't much deserve an exclamation point.) It feels silly to write about. But for me back then, it was silly in a very good way. It was euphorically silly. Previously, in my entire life up to that point, outside the auspices of games of spin the bottle or truth or dare, I had made out with a *total* of five girls. Through three years of high school, I had made out with three girls. It didn't make any sense, what was happening. It was like I had woken up as a different person that morning. A more attractive person. Or like the girls in our school had been hypnotized or brainwashed or had their bodies taken over by a Sumerian demigod like Sigourney Weaver in *Ghostbusters*.

Because girls were just walking right up to me and kissing me. My fantasies effortlessly fulfilled. I made out with a girl under the boardwalk, sunlight streaming through cracks in the slats, and of course sang the Drifters' "Under the Boardwalk" to myself as we were doing it. I made out with a girl on top of a parked police car, splayed out prone on the hood, in the middle of a large crowd of people at eleven o'clock in the morning. (I'd like to think I was singing N.W.A.'s "Fuck tha Police" to myself as we were doing this, but it was more likely Steve Miller's "Take the Money and Run.") My head was spinning. I had no idea what was going on. Maybe that was the key—maybe the sun and the sand and the music and beer had put me in such a good-feeling, relaxed state that whatever tight, overthinking teenage nervousness I usually wore on my face had melted away and left me looking somehow miraculously sexual.

Needless to say, it had taken me much longer to reach this state than I would have wanted it to. Years and years longer.

All my close friends had had sex by that point. (Or at least, all my close friends had told me that they had had sex by that point. And I believed them.) It was no fun at all, being the last virgin among my group of friends. I walked around in fear all the time, tangible fear, that the conversation might come up. Anyone who had had sex, or even anyone who had not had sex but who everyone else thought had had sex, all these people held a trump card over me in any argument that turned sharp, a game-ending cudgel in any round of disses or snaps. God forbid there were girls around. At the mere mention of virginity, at the sound of the word, a wave of shameful guilt, like the feeling of being caught in a lie, would rise from my stomach to my head. I would wish I could dis-integrate.

I imagine you can relate to all this. Pretty standard teenage boy stuff, I'd think. And you were a very nice guy. We were friends, you and I. Friends of a sort. Friendly. (Forgive me for not being able to remember your last name. We haven't seen each other for twenty-two years. Perhaps it's better that way, too, in light of my writing publicly about this. I figure it's not such a big deal. But I realize that it is a sensitive sub-ject.) You were a year younger than I was, a sophomore. But we were in a class together. Mrs. Dacey's Spanish class, was it? You were a skater and sort of a goth. I remember a pair of European-looking canvas sneakers you had. And that you shaved the side of your head close and sometimes wore black nail polish. We bonded over mutual appreciation of the mu-sic of the Cure and shared a smoke sometimes at parties.

So, as I think and hope you would understand, there was no way I was going to let the opportunity to have sex with your girlfriend pass by. She was the last of the five girls I made out with that day at the beach. We found ourselves standing next to each other in the crowd, whooping and cheering and holding beers aloft in salute to Joan Jett and the Blackhearts—who I swear sounded like reckless youth and joy personified up on that stage singing "I Hate Myself for Loving You"—and the next thing I knew we were kissing, and when we broke for air, I told her she should meet me at Chris Pack's house that night, where there had been a party in effect since the night of the prom because Chris was a senior about to graduate and his parents were out of town for the week.

Regardless of my quest to lose my virginity, though, and the all-day drunk I was on, and whether or not you'd understand my desperate thinking, this was a shitty thing for me to do. I knew she was your girlfriend. Everyone knew. She'd just moved to the area that year, had only been going to our school for a few months. She was very pretty—a blonde, big-haired rocker who wore tie-dye Zeppelin T-shirts and got a lot of attention from the harder-partying group of senior dudes that ran the commons area—and the fact that you, a quiet sophomore, had so quickly won her hand had boosted your rep along the locker-lined hallways. Judging from the expression on your face as you and she walked around together, you were aware of all of this.

When she showed up at Chris Pack's house, I met her

outside and led her to a romantic spot I found next to the neighbor's hedges, where we lay on the ground and split a beer and kissed again. She asked me not to tell anyone. She mentioned you and swore she never did stuff like this. Then we got up and went in to the party and, after a while, went upstairs to Chris's room. This was a crazy mind trip for me, because I had spent a great deal of time in this very room when I was younger, trading baseball cards and playing Dungeons & Dragons for hours upon hours upon days upon nights, but Chris and I had grown apart through adolescence, and I had not been there in three or four years.

She and I stretched out on Chris's bed, which was more comfortable than the ground beneath the hedges outside and also more comfortable than the hood of a police car or the trash-strewn sand under the boardwalk. We kissed some more and took off some of our clothes and writhed around on the sheets with increasing intensity, but when I tried to get my hand inside her underpants, she stopped me. "I'm on the rag," she said, sounding honestly disappointed.

I was disappointed, too, of course. Gauging by the writhing and our seminudity and by the general aura of sun-kissed blessedness that this long, long, wonderful day had taken on by this point, I had come to believe that perhaps my big moment had arrived. (It was as if some cosmic roll of two twenty-sided dice five years before had determined my fate and led me to this place at this time, and I was about to draw the sword from the stone and claim Camelot. Chris had a D&D character who was a wizard named Merlin. I realize that drawing the sword *from* the stone has this analogy anatomically backward.) But what could I do? I never wanted to be the type of guy who tried to cajole a girl into having sex. And even if I did want to, I wouldn't have known what to say. Begging for pity didn't seem like a good strategy.

So I just figured that I should keep doing what I was doing. Maybe she would give me a blow job. I'd never gotten one of those, either. Again, it didn't feel quite right to ask.

We started kissing again and writhing and groping, and after another ten minutes she rolled herself on top of me and whispered all breathy into my ear, "If I didn't have a tampon in, I'd totally fuck you right now."

Had I not been in such a drunken daze, I'm sure I would have burst out in some giggly exclamation of shock. (Or in an even more disappointingly premature way.) No one had ever said anything like that to me before. She was obviously much more experienced in these matters than I was. But I kept my composure. The possibility of sex seemed so close, closer by far than it had ever seemed before. I couldn't let it slip away.

"You know," I said, trying to sound like someone who had definitely had sex before. "*I don't mind*. If you wanted to take it out..."

She thought for a minute and shook her head, and we went back to kissing. Then she stopped and said, "Fuck it," and got up and put her shirt on and walked out to the bathroom.

How to describe my thoughts in the few minutes she was gone? Like I wanted to call everyone I'd ever met and sing them the chorus of "We Are the Champions," I guess. It's a good thing cell phones had not yet been invented.

When she came back in, I had a moment of guilty pause: Chris's sheets, it would be impolite to leave a mess. I mentioned this, and when she took her shirt off again, we laid it flat on the bed. Then she took off her shorts; then I took off my jeans. Then I had sex for the very first time in my life on top of a tie-dye Zeppelin T-shirt. Which still makes me smile when I think about it.

But this part doesn't make me smile: back at school on Monday, after the bell rang to change classes between fifth and sixth periods, as I was collecting my books and getting ready to leave Mr. Ganz's chemistry class, you walked into the room with an expression on your face very different from the one that had been there over the prior couple months.

I knew we weren't going to fight. I was not a fighter. You didn't seem like one, either. But I knew you had come there to see me, and I knew why. You walked right up and asked me if anything had happened.

"Were you kissing her on the beach?"

You winced when you said it, and your voice cracked a little. You knew. People had seen us, people told you.

I waited too long before answering and played cool guy more than I wish I had.

"That's a question you're gonna have to ask her," I said and picked up my books and walked away.

■ ■ ■

Dear Deb,

Sorry for making you take all those waterlogged maxi-pads and tampons off my car.

You were only ten. I was seventeen and a new driver. I'd bought an eight-year-old, metallic-blue Toyota Corolla from our dad's friend Alice for a dollar. It was a junker—rusted doors, yellow foam cushions poking through ripped vinyl seats, trunk that flew open around corners sometimes—but I invested $180 in a new carburetor, and it ran well enough to help me deliver Danny's pizzas in the summer and get me to school every morning that fall.

Of course, a teenage boy's first car offers other advantages, too. And mine earned the mostly joking, not-very-original nickname of "the Pussy Wagon" from two platonic girl-friends, Jennifer and Betsy, after I was lucky enough to have an early sexual experience in the backseat. (The episode be-came slightly famous among my circle of friends because Matt McCabe had come knocking on the fogged-up win-dow, asking if there was a person there. "Yes!" I told him. "Go away!" He knocked again. "Dave, it's Matt. Is there a per-son there?" I could have killed him. "Yes!" I shouted. "Fuck off!" He knocked again, asked again. Was he deaf? Was this a prank? Did he want me to tell him her name? I stopped what I was doing, clambered into the front seat, and opened the door a crack. "What the fuck, man?!" He was standing there with his girlfriend, Mary, who I'd driven to the party we were parked outside. "Sorry, Dave," Mary said. "But is my *purse* in there?")

A couple months later, on Mischief Night, the night before Halloween, Jennifer and Betsy played a good trick on me by decorating the car with fake cardboard license plates stenciled "P-WAGON" and a truly impressive number of maxipads and tampons, which they stuck all over the exterior using the little adhesive strips on the back of the maxipads and tape for the tampons. They were very thorough. There must have been five hundred maxipads on there. Fewer tampons, but you couldn't see much metallic blue.

Dad found it in our driveway in the morning and enjoyed the joke. He was good about things like that. I got a ride to school with someone else and congratulated Jennifer and Betsy when I saw them. The problem started the next day, when Dad asked me when I was going to remove the feminine hygiene products from the already-less-than-attractive car that was parked, for all to see, in front of his house.

Like many teenage boys, I was extremely squeamish about all things related to menstruation—a position that, thinking back on it, was largely put on. I thought guys were supposed to be that way, all freaked out and uncomfortable at the first mention of a girl's period; I associate this with Scott Valentine, the actor who played Mallory Keaton's boyfriend Nick on *Family Ties*. I think he got the heebie-jeebies about the subject one episode, and I don't know, I guess I thought he was cool. The way he said *Yo* all the time and stuff. (This goes pretty far toward explaining why I hadn't had sex earlier than I did. It was hard growing up in the '80s.) Anyway, I adopted that stance and refused to touch the pads and tampons. I told Dad I would make Jennifer and Betsy do it. He shook his head, disappointed.

Then it rained.

I had no idea how absorbent those things are! The pads ballooned to the size of bricks—like giant sodden baby diapers. The tampons were like dog bones, plumes of cotton exploding out of their thin cardboard tubes. My car looked like a quilted Stay Puft Marshmallow Man. It was way more disgusting. Dad was way more insistent about it being cleaned up. I was way less happy about the notion. And Jennifer and Betsy just laughed and laughed.

The rain stopped. Days passed. The stuff stayed inflated—like those aspirin-sized capsules that blow up into foam dinosaurs when kids put them in a bowl of water. (Magic!) This was their new shape.

"What's the big deal?" you said, far more reasonable at age ten than I was at seventeen. "It's just paper."

Being my little sister, you were always looking for opportunities to score points with me. I don't mean that in a way that implies fakeness. You were naturally cheery and effervescent and far less lazy than I ever was. Your disposition matched the sunny freckles on your face. (Those freckles were on my face, too. But in high school, I would have scrubbed them off with sandpaper if I could have.) I took advantage of your eagerness to please and, rising just above the level of a Tom Sawyer–style swindle, gave you a dollar for what must have been an hour's work on a Saturday.

This is perhaps a good time to make a blanket apology for my behavior as an older sibling. Much of it lacked in kindness and generosity: The time when you ordered a Miss Piggy sandwich at the sandwich shop in Truro because Miss Piggy was your favorite character on *The Muppets*, and I told you that they'd named it that because the ham in the sandwich was cut from the corpse of Miss Piggy herself. (That is sort of why they named it that, I suppose. But you were only five.) The time Chris Pack and I used you as a human shield during that rock fight in our driveway with Ryan Mingo and Michael Peterson. The time I told you not to talk to me for the entire four-hour drive to Boston. Oh, and I stole your Pogues CD. (Only *Hell's Ditch*, not one of their best. But that song "Lorca's Novena" is on there, with that killer bass line. I still have it. I was just listening to it, in fact.) I'll bet you can remember other stuff, too. My general air of dismissiveness. I always took family relationships for granted, too willing to put the notion of unconditional love to the test. And you're so much younger than I am. I never treated you as well as I should have.

You did a good job that day. When Dad got home, he was pleased to see the car had been cleaned. He thanked me. Then, after hearing I'd had you do it, shook his head again.

So, really, this is as much a thank-you as it is an apology. But I am sorry for being such a Scott Valentine and everything else. And you can have your Pogues CD back if you want.

■ ■ ■

Dear Bon Jovi,

Sorry for throwing empty beer cans on your lawn.

You know how sometimes you tell the day by the bottle that you drink, and then other times when you're alone and all you do is think? Well, sometimes when you're seventeen, and a world-famous rock star who is famously from the state where you live but whose music you strongly dislike buys a fancy house on a cul-de-sac in the next town over from yours, you find out where that house is and drive over there with a bunch of your friends and sit outside in your car and drink beer and throw the empty cans over the fence into the rock star's lawn. Like three times.

Kind of obnoxious, I realize, to start an apology by making fun of song lyrics you wrote almost twenty-five years ago. Though I do think they are incredibly bad. They are some of the worst lyrics to a rock song that I can think of. (Just after the ones from Kansas's "Carry On Wayward Son" about masquerading as a man with a reason and how that charade is the event of the season. Those are *the* worst.)

But I didn't intend this to be a critique of your lyrics. Whatever my opinion of them, it's no excuse for vandalism.

The fact is, I think it's wrong to throw empty beer cans, or any other trash, on another person's lawn under pretty much any circumstances. Even if that person surely has a well-paid grounds crew on hand to pick them up. Especially in that case, really, when you think about it. It's not like the guys in your grounds crew wrote "Wanted Dead or Alive" or "Livin' on a Prayer" or titled their album *Slippery When Wet*.

Jesus, this must be the least apologetic-sounding apology you've ever gotten. Obviously, I'm still conflicted about your contribution to my home state's cultural image. You know, you titled your next album *New Jersey*. A couple years from now, I'll probably be writing you another apology just for the tone of this one. So before I fall into some kind of infinite regression, allow me to be sincere again.

While I believe very much in forgiving youthful indiscretion, including my own, I also believe in taking responsibility for one's actions. It was my idea to drive there, to park there, to throw the first can. There were often a couple other cars parked there, too. Your real fans, I assumed, hoping for a chance at an autograph. There was a Camaro there once, and I wondered whether its inhabitants would be hurt or angry, would perhaps want to fight us when they saw what we were doing. I felt a twinge of guilt then for the snobbish insult to them, to their taste. But not about what I was doing to you, the rock star. I wish I had thought then as I do now: no matter how famous someone is, no matter how I might feel about the music someone makes, that someone is an actual person. He actually lives in that house, and this is not cool.

And you're probably a really good person. I've never heard otherwise. In fact, this past summer when I was back in New Jersey for the weekend, I ran into an old friend of mine, Kevin Krosnick, who told me you'd been doing a lot of charity work lately with his father, who is a doctor, an oncologist, who I know to be a good person because he helped my family when my father got sick. Apparently, you've been helping a lot of people that don't have health insurance to get medical treatment. This is an unmitigated good, regardless of the quality of the lyrics of any given song. Sorry again. I just can't let the lyrics thing go. Maybe you'd even agree at this point, though, huh? I mean, it's okay, right? Lyrics are just one element of a song. A small part, really, of your job. You're forty-eight, I'm almost forty. Everything is more complex than we think it is when we're kids, right? And it's not like admitting that—because, I mean, they're kind of perfect in their way, too. For a silly, pubescent, rock star–outlaw-cowboy thing. Like Foreigner's "Juke Box Hero," too, right? I loved that song when I was twelve. Or Bob Seger's "Turn the Page"—that must have been a big influence, right? I would have been the biggest Bon Jovi fan going if "Wanted Dead or Alive" had come out three years earlier than it did. In fact, I really liked the first song of yours that I ever heard, "Runaway," which did come out three years earlier, in 1983— you had won a local battle of the bands 103.5 WAPP held, right? I heard it at the 7-Eleven, waiting on line to play *Ms. Pac-Man*. That dynamite keyboard line and then your voice comes in talking about streets and girls and social lives.

It fit the scene just right. I still like that song! But even if you did agree with me about the problems with the lyrics to "Wanted Dead or Alive," even if you chuckled and said, "Yeah, you know, thinking back, I have to admit, pretty ridiculous," that wouldn't change the fact that this song, this thing you thought of with your brain, is inarguably a classic. Get in a car anywhere, drive around for an hour listening to the radio, and you'll hear it—New Jersey and Long Island, of course, but California and South Carolina, too. Almost twenty-five years since it came out, your song gets played on the radio, how many times every day? Hundreds? Thousands? How many classic rock stations are there in the country? It must be very satisfying. Not to mention the money it's made you. I don't say this to be a dick. You deserve that money. It's a very catchy song, eminently sing-alongable with, especially the part where Richie echoes you in the chorus, when he makes *wanted* into a four-syllable word. Everybody loves to sing that part. Everybody fights over it at karaoke. You know this. You wrote that melody with your brain. Surely you know how so many people love it. You've toured all over the world, performed it in front of millions of fans—you rocked all their faces, you said. I'm sorry, I can't help it. Those lyrics! God, they're so ridiculous, right?! You know it, too, right?! I mean, come on! You must know it. You must laugh about it, right? You and Richie and Heather or Denise or whoever he's hanging out with at the moment. I'm sorry, I'm being a dick again. I don't know what it's like to be famous. But, man, the guitar-as-gun metaphor? And calling your tour bus a horse? Ha-ha-ha-ha! Right?! But it's okay! It doesn't matter. No matter how silly I think those lyrics are, no matter how much they make me laugh my snotty laugh, I know them all by heart. In fact, I've come to love them in a way. In a confusing and complicated way. In a way perhaps not entirely unlike the way you can feel sort of proud about some dumb thing you did when you were a drunk punk kid, even as you know and are fully willing to admit that it was wrong and so are, at the same time, honestly ashamed of it. That song is a part of me. It's a part of New Jersey. The culture. A part of our state's big, stinky, stupid, romantic, gorgeous, ugly, profound, cheesy swamp. And you wrote it.

What did I ever do? I threw empty beer cans over a fence.

■ ■ ■

Dear Mom,

Sorry for choosing *Hannah and Her Sisters* when you asked me to go out and rent some movies for our family to watch to get our minds off the fact that Dad had been diagnosed with cancer.

You remember, I'm sure, that this was just a couple weeks before I graduated from high school. It must have been a weekend because we were all at home in the afternoon. Dad walked into the TV room with his friend David Landy. You could tell that David Landy had been crying.

"The doctor just hit me with it," Dad said. "Boom." His eyes looked like they weren't really looking at us, and his voice sounded like it was coming from far away. But he said he thought that the doctor had done the right thing. "So I'm just gonna hit you with it."

The cancer had started in his lung. At least that's what they thought. It was hard to tell. By the time anybody knew anything, it had spread to his brain and his lymph nodes and his spinal column and everywhere. *Metastasized* was the unfamiliar word. The doctor had told him that he would be dead in two months.

We sat in the TV room for a long time with the TV off.

Deb cried. I went upstairs and looked at myself in my bathroom mirror. I looked normal, but I felt like a different person. Like the person who I was when I'd woken up that morning was no more and that this new person that I had become was hidden inside my head, looking out through fake eye sockets at this thing in the mirror that was only a shell. Why wasn't I crying? Why didn't I even feel like crying? Shouldn't a person be crying after learning that one's father is dying? It felt like a dream, like I'd wake up the next day and this wouldn't be happening.

But I knew it was real and that it was a big deal. One that I felt wholly unprepared for, despite the fact that Dad had come into the kitchen a few weeks prior and asked me to get off the phone so we could talk and endured the put-upon expression I fixed him with to tell me that he was having some medical tests. He'd said that he'd been coughing up blood and that he didn't know why and that it might be serious. It might be bad, he'd said. He hadn't said the word *cancer*, though, and I had quickly pushed it out of my mind and not given it much more thought. Because I was so good at being what sitcoms and movies had taught me teenagers were supposed to be like and convincing myself that you and Dad didn't mean anything to me.

"Dad has cancer." I said it out loud to myself. "Dad is dying."

I stood there for a moment, blinking, wondering if this would jog me into a burst of emotion that felt more real.

"This is what it feels like when your dad is dying," I said.

I wrote Dad a clumsy note to tell him that I loved him. "You're like Superman to me," I wrote. I didn't know what else to write. I went into your room and tucked the note under the pillow on his side of the bed. The house was quiet.

Later, back down in the TV room, Dad told us he was going to fight the cancer as hard as he could. Despite what the doctor had told him, he was determined to do whatever it took to beat it. "I've been a fighter all my life," he said. "I'm not going to quit now."

He came over to where I was sitting on the arm of the couch and looked me hard in the eye. "I'm gonna need you here with me on this one," he said. "Don't run away from me. I need you here with me and as part of this family. And I need you *present*. Don't go and hide in the bottom of a bottle or inside the tube of a bong." I told him I wouldn't.

Dad's parents drove down from West Orange. Thea was

crying as she walked in the door, tissues already crumpled into balls in her hands, her face twisted into an expression that made it hard to imagine that she would ever be able to smile again. Pa looked stooped and older than he'd ever looked before.

At dinnertime, no one felt much like eating. I forget if it was you or David Landy who had the idea that we should rent some movies to watch, but I thought it was a good one. Get our minds off the news, lighten the mood to the extent that that might be possible. I remember Dad agreed and that he said to get comedies. "I want to laugh," he said.

I volunteered to go to the video store. I wanted to get out of the house, out of that atmosphere, even if only for twenty minutes. I liked feeling that I was helping, too, even in a minor way. Alone in the carport, once the door closed behind me, I took what felt like my first full breath in hours.

Soft-rugged and fluorescent lit, the video store gave me the same dissociative feeling as looking in the mirror had. There I was in this very familiar place, a place where I'd spent so many hours of my life doing exactly what I was doing then, scanning the collection, searching for titles that I knew or new ones that looked intriguing, a place where there were always faces I recognized—Ms. Maxwell, an English teacher at my school, worked there some nights—a place where people met and stopped to chat. There I was, just like always, except not at all like always. Walking around the store, I couldn't help thinking about what I looked like to the other people around me. I saw Mr. Johnson, Jeremy's dad, there that night. Did he recognize me? Did I seem the same? I suppose I did. I wasn't trembling or sobbing or breathing into a brown paper bag; there wasn't blood dripping from my nose or soaking through my shirt from my chest. I was just standing there, my jaw set firm, squinting slightly as I scanned the titles on the plastic-sheathed spines of the VHS boxes on one of the racks in the comedy section. I felt like a spy. I felt like a liar.

I don't know how exactly it happened. I guess I was caught up in thinking about this stuff, in a sort of daze, as I was choosing videos. I got *A Fish Called Wanda* and, I think, *Porky's*, which was always a favorite of Dad's and mine. And then I found *Hannah and Her Sisters*. It's weird because I had seen that movie before. We all had and liked it. We were big Woody Allen fans. But in remembering that we liked it, and in the daze I was in without really knowing I was in it, I forgot that one of the main plotlines of that movie revolves around Woody Allen's character believing he has a brain tumor.

I stopped on the way home to pick up my girlfriend. I had told her the news and asked that she come over.

When we got back to our house and got out of the car, she saw the bag from the video store and asked me what I had rented. When I told her *Hannah and Her Sisters*, she stopped suddenly. "We can't go in there with that movie," she said. She reminded me what happens to Woody Allen's character.

"Oh my god," I gasped. We were standing in the carport. "How could I have forgotten that?"

I cursed myself and shook my head. I felt like someone who has been hypnotized onstage, awakening to the sound of the magician's finger snap, looking around to see who's watching. It was frightening—one of those moments when your trust in your own judgment falters.

Thank god she had stopped me. Thank god I hadn't gotten inside and popped it into the VCR. "Hey, is everybody ready to laugh?! This movie is about someone who thinks he has cancer!"

I didn't know what to do. She said we should go back and pick a different movie. I opened the door quietly and called you over from the TV room where everyone was waiting. "Here," I said, handing you the two other movies. "You can start watching one. I have to go back to the store."

You looked at me quizzically. "Why? What happened?"

I showed you the box for *Hannah and Her Sisters*. "Woody Allen's character is a hypochondriac who thinks he has cancer."

"Oh." Your voice fell. "Oh."

"I...I don't know what I was thinking," I stuttered. "I forgot."

"Yes..." You tried to be comforting. "I would like to think that Dad could find that funny right now, but I don't think he could."

I closed the door behind me. I don't know what you told everyone about where I was going. I think you started *A Fish Called Wanda*.

■ ■ ■

Dear Dr. Nogueira,

I'm sorry for slipping a beer cap into your hand when you gave me my diploma at graduation.

It was such a stupid thing to do. A very immature sort of prank and not very original. Though by the confused expression on your face as I did it, I'm guessing that you'd never had it pulled on you—and you'd been principal of Red Bank Regional High School for eleven years.

It was a warm but gray day in early June. Many of us in the class of 1989 had spent the two hours before our graduation ceremony at my friend Ted's house. His family had an old barn on their property with a loft that had been converted into a studio apartment that was the site of lots of parties during high school, and we'd all gathered there to drink beer and smoke pot before this important rite of passage. Earlier in the day, at the last practice session before the real thing, a plan had been hatched. Andy Callahan, always a fun-loving mischief maker, had heard of a thing that some other high school students had done in the past: as the graduates were called up one by one to receive their diplomas and the traditional congratulatory shake of the principal's hand, they'd all given him a beer cap they'd been palming on their approach to the podium. The idea was that the principal, not wanting to disrupt the ceremony, would have to slip the caps into his pocket. But if all went according to plan, if a critical mass of participants was achieved, his pockets would fill with caps and he'd have to just start dropping them on the ground, where a visible pile would form and hilarity would ensue. I really liked the sound of this prank, as it spoke to anti–school spirit and announced to the world the very important fact that high school students liked to drink beer. Word spread, and we all promised we'd do it. It was going to be great!

By way of explanation but not of excuse, I will tell you that my father was sick with cancer. A first round of chemotherapy had laid him flat, and he couldn't get out of bed to come watch me graduate. Looking back, I can see that I may have been partying with extra abandon at this time of my life, caring less if I was to be arrested or get in a car crash or something, with the thought that this would make a dramatic plot development in the novel that I saw as my life. Everybody sees their life like that to a certain extent, right? Especially when we're teenagers. Even though it's wrong and unhealthy. Also, it's hard to say that my behavior would have been any different if my father had not gotten sick. I was living in much the same way before it happened—I consoled myself with this fact whenever I thought about a promise I'd made to my father to not "hide" from him with drink and drugs. I'd been getting drunk and high all the time before his diagnosis; nothing had changed. It's easy to rationalize things to your own conscience. I could still look him in the eye over dinner every night. I'd yet to cry about his having cancer; yet to feel like crying even. I was still in shock maybe. I don't know. Regardless, I don't want to accept it as an excuse. Plenty of people have bad things happen in their lives. Not everyone acts like a schmuck.

So at the barn, as the time approached to leave to go graduate, as we chugged our last beers and smoked our last bowls
in the warmth of four years' worth of comradery, Andy and
I and a couple of others went around making sure everyone
had kept a bottle cap with which to execute the hilarious
prank. "It's only going to work if we all remember to do it,"
we told people. And I accepted a ride to the ceremony, not
with my best friends Mark and Ted, nor my girlfriend, but
with some other friends, less close friends, who had offered
me some cocaine to snort on the way.

I'd tried cocaine a couple of times before. But only a couple. So it was still a new thrill—and, as everyone in the car
impressed upon me, a big serious secret—when we pulled
into the parking lot of the church on Tower Hill and passed
around a newly published Red Bank Regional yearbook with
white lines of powder cut on the vinyl-smooth cover. We
drove around for a while and stopped once more for another
bump before pulling up to the school and floating into the
gym, where most of our class had already assembled.

Two hundred and forty-two kids pulling gowns on over
their clothes, finding their place in the procession. Teachers
and vice principals and guidance counselors pointing directions, shouting instructions. I wandered around the crowd,
not bothering to find my spot, looking up at the ceiling in
the gym, imagining the perspective from up in the rafters,
where the basketball banners hung. It must have looked
silly—the hustle-bustle, the formality, all this dolling up, for
meaningless tradition. For nothing. I smiled to myself, feel-

ing above it all. No one else could see what I could see. No one else knew what I knew.

Mark stopped me as I wandered past him. "Breeze," he said, like snapping his fingers. "Breeze." (My nickname in high school was "Breezer" because the *y* in my last name is pronounced with the long *e* sound, like Brie cheese. Perhaps you remember this? I would be impressed. Regardless, I did not choose the nickname and will not take responsibility for it.)

There was concern in Mark's eyes. "Breeze, you all right?"

"Yeah," I said, trying to relax my smile. "I got a great buzz goin'."

I collected myself and put on my gown and went to my spot in line and tried to get my mortarboard cap to tilt just the way Robert Downey Jr.'s did in *Less Than Zero*. Then we all marched through the roll-up garage doors at the side of the gym, out to the football field where all the white folding chairs were arranged facing the stage and the podium and the bleachers behind them. My mom was sitting in those bleachers and my little sister and my grandmother, Thea. But so were some two thousand other people, and I couldn't make out their faces from my seat.

What happened during the ceremony? People gave speeches? You? The valedictorian of our class? Who was that? Mary Jude Cox? She was always so smart and also very nice, but I don't remember anything she said that day. Did someone sing? The school band played "Pomp and Circumstance"? I wasn't paying a lot of attention. I was gazing off into the sky and looking up at the crowd in the stands, thinking how funny it was that they were all there watching us, watching me, but from so far away. They'd all come thinking this was such a big important day for us, and here I was as high as I was and glad to not be caring about anything.

It felt like a villain's victory. And at one point I considered doing something to disrupt the ceremony, to make a big ridiculous mockery of it all—shout out a profanity, strip naked and run around like a crazy person. There was definitely something attractive about that: going out in a ball of fire in front of a big audience. But I would have never done it. Not just me alone certainly. I was never that brave. I might have liked the idea of shocking people—Keith Moon driving a Rolls-Royce into a hotel swimming pool—but if I was honest with myself, I could never get over the fact that, when it came down to it, I wanted people to like me. Ruining graduation, making a big show of it, that was beyond me. I would have to settle for the subtle bottle cap prank.

I did take my hat off and throw it up in the air long before I was supposed to. The hat throwing was the part of the ceremony I was most looking forward to. (Well, besides the bottle cap prank.) Everyone knows the graduating class is supposed to throw their hats in the air at the end of the show. Everyone has seen the videos. I'd always thought it was cool how aerodynamic the mortarboard shape was—those things can really fly like Frisbees if you angle them right.

At one point in the proceedings, deep into the proceedings, but before we'd been called by name to get our diplomas, the excitement level rose. Whatever the person at the podium was saying (was it you? I think it might have been), whatever whoever was speaking was saying was eliciting big applause from both the crowd in the stands and my classmates around me. You were or someone else was talking about the accomplishment of completing high school and how we should be proud of ourselves and stuff. And just as I fully tuned in, you or someone else said, "Congratulations to Red Bank Regional's class of nineteen eighty-nine!" Everyone clapped and cheered. I thought that was our cue. I wanted to get rowdy; I was eager to get those caps flying. I took mine off my head, let out a hearty *"whoo-hoo!"* and flung it skyward.

It was a pretty good throw, twenty feet high or so, and I enjoyed watching it cut the air in a graceful downward arc and land on the running track to the left of the stage. All by itself. I realized my mistake when no one else followed my lead.

So I waited, hatless, through the rest of the speech. A few minutes later, it was time for us all to stand. Someone else stepped to the microphone and started reading out our names. I reached under my gown and into my pants pocket and grasped the bottle cap. We filed behind the last row of chairs, and down an aisle to the left of the stage like we had done in practices, and one by one, crossed in front of our classmates and took our turns striding up to where you were standing in your fancier cap and gown with its colorful sash and gold piping. I got to the edge of the stage and heard my name called and heard the clapping and cheers from the crowd—my family, my friends' families, teachers, and school staff, I suppose, some genuinely happy for me, others perhaps just happy for me to go. I looked down at the ground next to you as I approached and saw no bottle caps. But I was pretty early in the procession, my last name beginning with B. I figured your pockets were not yet full. I grinned goofily when you said congratulations and handed me my diploma, and we shook hands and I palmed you the bottle cap. You received it wordlessly without looking down to check what it was. I watched your face for reaction. You were nonplussed. You knew what it was I'd given you, it seemed, but your expression said simply, "Why did you just give me a bottle cap?" Nothing more. You were also probably wondering why I wasn't wearing a hat.

I followed the person in front of me back to our chairs and sat and watched the rest of the class get their diplomas. Some people were really psyched, lifting their arms over their heads like boxing champions and stuff. Lots of big smiles. As more and more people shook your hand, I periodically leaned forward and looked to see if I could see a pile of bottle caps forming next to your feet. I never did.

You gave out the last diploma (to…Jen Yankowski?) and soon after the applause had died down and everyone was back seated, there was another address. (Was *this* when you gave yours?) This one was short, and this time when we heard the words, "Congratulations to Red Bank Regional's class of nineteen eighty-nine," everybody somehow knew it was the real thing and not a second false alarm. The caps flew en masse this time, like they were supposed to, falling like big black confetti. It was satisfying, and the cheers were louder than ever, and everyone was so happy. We were officially graduated.

Dizzying chaos on the football field as families flooded from the stands to greet their graduates. Mine found me and my mom snapped a picture of me standing and smiling with my sister and my grandmother. It came out nicely, the three us smiling, looking right into the camera. My mom hung it on the fridge in our kitchen at home, where it stayed all summer. Deb looked cute, Thea looked proud, and I looked fine, too—if a bit slack, my gown undone, no cap. But I never liked to look at it. I felt like I could see the drugs in my eyes, and the way I held my face said something fake. Even standing there with two people that I loved, there was an ugliness behind my smile. The thought that I was tricking people, getting one over on them. Sure, there I was posing. But I knew full well that what I was thinking about was how soon I could get back to Ted's to drink another beer, how I could hook up with the crew who had driven me to the ceremony so I could get more cocaine. I definitely wanted more cocaine. Even as my grandmother kissed me on the cheek, leaving a lipstick mark you could see in the photo, what I was mostly thinking about was how to get more cocaine.

I would get some more later that night. Once everyone had finished their celebratory dinners with families at Italian restaurants or backyard barbecues and the teenage wasteland had reconvened at my old friend Dave's house, I got a tap on the shoulder and was told in a whisper that a surprise had been left for me under a lace doily in the pink, potpourri-scented, floral-print bathroom off the kitchen—right near the pantry I'd been pulling Double Stuf Oreo cookies out of since the fourth grade. It all felt so dark and depraved. It was just what I wanted. I was up all night that night, and I didn't tell anyone about it. Not even my girlfriend when I went back to her house.

Earlier, though, a bunch of us were sitting around a table on the back deck. Andy was there and Mark and Ted and Kevin Krosnick. I asked for a report on the success of the prank. Had anybody seen any beer bottle caps amassing at your feet? Had you said anything to anybody as the numbers you'd been handed continued to rise?

"Oh, I didn't do it," someone said.

"Neither did I."

"I forgot."

"I don't think anybody did," Andy said casually. "I think pretty much everybody pussied out."

"What?" I said. "I did it!"

"You did?" Kevin's eyes bugged. "What did Nogueira do?"

"Nothing. He just took it."

"Oh, man," Andy said, cracking up. "I didn't think anybody did it. It didn't seem right once you got up there. It just felt wrong."

It should have.

■ ■ ■

Dear Mark,

Sorry for getting tears and snot and probably a little puke all over your shirt.

This was soon after you and I had graduated high school. We were in the barn at Ted's house very late at night—or, really, very early in the morning. The sun was coming up. There had been a party there, like there had been most nights that summer, but we were the last two people left. Ted had staggered off to bed in the main house.

For some reason, before we collapsed onto the couch or the floor or attempted to stagger back to our respective houses, we decided to chug one more beer. This turned out to be a bad idea.

I forget what we said as we clinked our plastic cups. I forget whether we said anything at all. But I know we were standing by the fridge by the stairs, and immediately after I'd gulped mine down, I went into the bathroom and puked it right up. Along with lots more of the beer I'd drunk that night.

No big deal. It was not at all uncommon for one of our crowd to puke up beer at the end of a night. But that night, or that morning, in the bathroom at the barn as I pushed myself up off my knees, it became a big deal. Standing but not steadily, I looked out the window above the toilet. I saw the pale dawn light of the sky and the leaves of the maple trees that grew out back, and I thought of my father, who was lying in bed at my house, his skin the color of yellow chalk, recovering from chemotherapy. He had been lying in bed like that, mostly unconscious, for two weeks.

It's not that I hadn't been thinking about this. I had been thinking about it a lot. I had been opening his bedroom door every day and peeking in. We weren't supposed to get too close because his immune system was compromised, but I could see that his hair was falling out and his muscles were shriveling faster than I would have thought those things could have happened.

It's not even that I hadn't been talking about it. I'd been talking about it with my mom—a colleague of hers had had a husband die after being diagnosed with terminal cancer a few years earlier, and she had told my mom that the best thing to do was to accept the fact that the sick person was going to die, to accept this as early in the process as possible, and to do the grieving then. (Not in front of the sick person, of course, who is relying on hope to fuel his fight.) Then all the time you get with the person beyond that is like a bonus, and the death itself will come as a softer blow. She thought this made sense, my mom, and I did, too. We also worried that my dad might die very soon, imminently, from the side effects of the chemotherapy treatment. That happened sometimes apparently. And he certainly looked like he was dying. I'd been talking about it with my girlfriend, too, whose own mom had died of cancer when she was nine— we talked about it a lot. She was very good to talk to. But I hadn't been talking much about it to you or Ted or Chris or Matt or Dave. I hadn't been talking much about it to guys.

I turned around from the toilet and looked at my reflection in the mirror over the sink. Panting, puffy, pukey saliva drooling down my chin—I was a picture I did not like to see. My face quivered and seemed to crack, and I realized I was losing control of myself.

There were tears in my eyes when I walked back into the main room, back to where you were near the fridge by the stairs, and I stood in front of you, and when I saw that you saw the tears in my eyes, I stumbled forward and fell into your chest. You wrapped your long, basketball-player arms all the way around me and held me. My knees buckled and I collapsed and you held me up. You took my full weight as I sank into you and sobbed and sobbed and let you hold me in a way that I hadn't let anyone hold me, not my mom or my dad, not my girlfriend or anyone else, in a long, long time.

At some point, I lifted my head from your shirt, your soaked and mucousy shirt. "I'm a pussy," I blubbered. "I'm a fucking pussy."

"You're not a pussy." You patted my head and talked soft sense. "No one thinks you're a pussy. None of us can call you a pussy because none of us has gone through what you're going through."

I cried harder and harder, emptying myself. You went on.

"If anything, we're the pussies," you said. "Because we all want to say something, but none of us know what to say."

So this is more of a thank-you than an apology, I guess. For being a good friend, for making me feel better. But, you know, I am sorry about your shirt.

COLLEGE

(Or the six longest years of my life.)

Dear Todd Schwartz and Chris McGuire,

Sorry for spilling fruit punch all over the box of Calvin and Hobbes T-shirts you were hoping to sell.

It was the first semester of our freshman year of college, on the second floor of Marshall Dormitory, in the prison-cell-like, cinder-block room you two shared with a guy named Scott. I lived down the hall, in a similar room with my roommates Sean and Jeremy.

We'd only known each other for a month or so. We'd only known anybody we knew there for a month or so. And probably because we were all trying too hard to make people like us, you guys decided to invest some money in printing up a line of the familiar comic-strip-characters-acting-naughty T-shirts that were so popular on college campuses at the time. (*Are they still so popular?* I wonder.) You recruited another guy in our dorm, Jeff, a talented sketch artist, to draw a facsimile of Bill Watterson's Calvin and Hobbes drinking alcohol. It was a business venture. You weren't trying to break any new ground.

What should the shirts say, though? What clever slogan to best represent our college and our wit? We all pitched in with ideas. I forget who came up with the winner, but I'm happy to think that it was not me.

"Connecticut College," the shirts were to say on the front, with a picture of Calvin and Hobbes laughing with cans of beer in their hands. Under the picture were the words "When It's Night Out..." Then on the back of the shirt, the pair would be depicted lying prone, with X marks in their eyes, under the punch line: "We BLACK Out!!!"

You brought the design to a silk screener at the Crystal Mall and put in an order for two hundred shirts for four hundred dollars. You planned to sell them for ten dollars each.

A couple weeks later, the shipment arrived in a cardboard box the size of a large television set. Many of us on our floor bought one the very first day. We were being friendly, supporting you in your endeavor. I wish I could say that's as far as my support went, but I actually wore the shirt a few times—once when my parents and eleven-year-old sister had come to visit. My father was sick, and as I remember his tired, defeated tone when he voiced his disapproval—"Why would you want to wear a shirt like that?"—well, this apology isn't just to you.

Credit to our fellow students' taste, the T-shirts did not sell like hotcakes. You guys unloaded maybe twenty more in the following days, but after that, the mostly full box of product sat in your room next to Todd's bunk.

Also living in our dorm that year were a group of sophomores we looked up to and hoped to befriend. From time to time they would mix up a punch made with Kool-Aid and grain alcohol in an orange Gatorade cooler and serve it, for some reason, out of a plastic decoy duck someone had brought to school. They did this in the hallway this night, and we joined them, and I drank too much. (Which really, when it comes to drinking grain alcohol punch out of a plastic duck decoy, is pretty much the point.) One of the sophomore guys, Carter, drank too much, too. And at some point, unluckily for you, the party migrated from the hallway into your room. And because we were having trouble standing, Carter and I found ourselves sitting on the big cardboard box, cackling like the type of fools who would wear T-shirts that say, "When it's night out, we black out." Then we started pouring full cups of the punch over each other's heads. The alcohol stung my eyes. I don't remember a lot more. Because, you know, it was night out...

The next day, we discovered that the punch had dripped through the box and soaked through the T-shirts, dyeing some solid, leaving even the least affected with a few small splotches of pink. All unsellable.

You guys were unhappy. But largely because of Carter's elder status, your loss was chalked up to collateral party damage. The shirts were your responsibility; you should have moved them or spread a tarp or something before allowing such obviously inebriated fun-loving innocents into your room. You'd made much of your money back already anyway. We'd mostly cost you potential profits.

In hindsight, the ruination of those god-awful T-shirts was a good thing for everybody, a good thing for the world. The less chance another sick, tired father would have to see his son wearing one, the better. But still, businesswise, I guess I owe you a couple of bucks.

■ ■ ■

Dear Visiting Music Professor Who Taught History of Jazz at Connecticut College, Spring Semester 1990,

I'm sorry for comparing Miles Davis's *Kind of Blue* to Bob Seger's "Turn the Page."

I can only imagine what your reaction was. You there, grading papers, sitting in your office, or at home in your apartment in New Haven—you were visiting from Yale. As part of a faculty exchange program, was it? So a professor from Connecticut College was up there, teaching your regular students at the time? (Man, you got the short end of that one, huh?) I picture you reading the little blue test booklet I'd turned in, going red in the face, then ripping the beret off your head and throwing it across the room. You never wore a beret in class, but I always assumed you put one on as soon as you got home.

It was our first assignment. We were to go to the listening library and listen to a selection of records from a list you'd handed out and write down our impressions. We were supposed to log six hours' worth. Due at the end of the second week of class.

I didn't know a thing about jazz. My dad had a lot of old jazz albums, but I listened to rock music and rap. I had signed up for the course because it sounded easy. I was not a good student. Still, I liked what I heard, sitting in the library cubicle with those big old-fashioned earphones on my head. One of the first records on the list was Miles Davis's *Kind of Blue*, the consensus "greatest jazz album of all time," a work many people would say stands at the very top of American musical achievement. Some would argue—and considering your field of study, I wouldn't be surprised if you are one of them—that it stands at the top of American artistic achievement of any kind.

Somehow, I doubt you feel similarly about Bob Seger's classic-rock radio standard, "Turn the Page." Frankly, I don't either. I've always thought of Seger as a poor man's Bruce Springsteen. A very poor man's. (Though I'll never be able to turn the dial when "Night Moves" comes on.) But hearing the mournful, haunting trumpet Davis plays on "Blue in Green" for the first time, my closest frame of reference was the mournful, haunting saxophone (all right, the cheesy, melodramatic saxophone) the Silver Bullet Band's Alto Reed played on "Turn the Page." So that's what I wrote. That was my impression. That was the assignment, right? (I Google searched to get Alto Reed's name, by the way. It is not his real one. His parents called him Thomas Neal Cartmell.)

Pressed to give my younger self a break, I can drum up a defense of "Turn the Page." Yes, it's a plodding, overserious account of a rocker's life on the road. There are lots like it. Journey's "Faithfully" comes to mind. And Bon Jovi basically rewrote it for "Wanted Dead or Alive." But the part where Seegs talks about feeling eyes on him as he walks into a restaurant, hearing snickered comments about his hair—"Is that a woman or a man?"—that's resonated with me since I was a seventh grader, brushing my own hair out of my face, keeping my finger on Record while I listened to 102.7 WNEW on my box. The song is very effective in its way. It caught something just right and, at least for a certain audience, stands the test of time. There's a reason Metallica chose to cover it twenty-five years after it was recorded, though I wish they hadn't.

But Seger also wrote "Like a Rock" from the Chevy commercials. That's enough to ruin anybody's day. He belongs in a conversation with Journey, Bon Jovi, and latter-day Metallica. Mentioning him alongside Miles Davis, in hindsight, is embarrassing. Comparing *Kind of Blue* to "Turn the Page" is sort of like looking at *Guernica* and saying it reminds you of *The Horse Whisperer*. Y'know, because of the horse.

Luckily for me, that first assignment wasn't graded. Unluckily for me, subsequent assignments were. And subsequent tests. I stopped attending your lectures after a few weeks. Class met at eleven o'clock in the morning, which conflicted with my sleep schedule at that point in my life. But I was also too stupid to get myself to the registrar's office and drop the course. So that June, after answering a very small percentage of the questions on the final exam and getting what I imagine to be only a small percentage of that percentage right, I became perhaps the first person in the history of college to actually fail History of Jazz.

PUBLIC APOLOGY

■ ■ ■

Dear High School Girlfriend,

Sorry for leaving all the letters you'd sent me in the bureau in my freshman-year dorm room.

I'd put them there with the intention of keeping them. But the day that my mom drove the car up from New Jersey, when I opened the drawer and saw all those pieces of paper, all scattered and crumpled with their half-torn envelopes, I didn't know how I would collect them all and get them into a bag. I was having trouble thinking clearly. I was severely hungover.

That's never a good excuse, I know. Especially as you and my mom had already helped me through so much of the day, packing up all my clothes and books and CDs and stuff, bringing everything downstairs and loading the trunk, while I lay in your bed. You had come to join me at Connecticut College that semester, because the previous one that fall, when I was there and you were at your school, a large mid-Atlantic state university, we'd missed each other with the type of it's-the-end-of-the-world, I-can't-breath-without-you desperation specific to teenagers.

God, the time we spent on the train that fall. Seven hours there and back, Amtrak's Metroliner, pretty much every other weekend. (I can still taste the Diamond brand smoked almonds they sell in the dining car.) And the time talking on the phone. I'd hunch myself into the tight wooden booth in the lobby of my dorm, pressing the receiver hard against my face, gasping ridiculous proclamations of subsumption and foreverness, aching at the sound of you crying, swearing I'd drop out and come down there and run away with you as soon as you gave the word. "Nothing else means anything to me," I told you while groups of my new classmates walked past laughing at what I was sure must have been some idiotic joke. As if it were not, in fact, the end of the world. And, of course, we spent a great deal of time writing each other letters. Lots and lots of letters. I got a letter from you every day. Sometimes two. There must have been over a hundred letters in that drawer.

You wrote me more letters than I wrote you. You were more miserable at your school than I was at mine. It must have been easier to feel lonely there, lost among sixteen thousand strange-faced students on a city campus. It was a big Greek scene there, and that wasn't your thing at all. Connecticut College was about the same size as our high school: 1,600 students on a campus like a pretty park. It was more manageable, much less intimidating. There were no fraternities or sororities.

I'd made a group of friends in my dorm, and you'd gotten to know and like them on visits that often and increasingly lasted three or four days. You were happier on your visits to Connecticut. I was happier when you were there. The obvious solution was to somehow get you up there to stay. We found out about the visiting student program and filled out the application as a first step to never spending another minute apart for the rest of our lives.

It was awesome when you got there. You were given a single room in the dorm right next to mine. We immediately pushed two mattresses together to make a king-size bed and were thus able to avoid the uncomfortable sleepover parties we'd foisted on our respective roommates the previous semester. (College is so weird.) I brought over some clothes and CDs and basically moved in. The other people on your floor were less pleased with the situation. You happened to have been put on an all-girls floor—a rarity at the college, which prided itself on its coed bathrooms—and one to which most of your neighbors had been assigned by request. It was a quiet, sober, clean-smelling floor, and while we got along well with the girl who lived directly next to us (what was her name? She had that pet tarantula I let crawl on my arm. Otto. Funny that I remember the spider's name and not hers. I bumped into her years later in the East Village. She was living backstage at a theater where Peter Arbour was directing a play. She was nice. Katie maybe?), your RA eventually alerted us that there had been anonymous complaints about my presence. We ignored these complaints on the grounds that it was 1990 and people should get over their Victorian era hang-ups. But that was not for us to decide, so they deserve an apology, too, the other girls in your hall.

You fit in well in my dorm, becoming friends with my friends easily, smoothly, in a way that made me proud. You joined in the teasing at the lunch table and the wasting of long afternoons watching *The Mod Squad* and *The Streets of San Francisco* in syndication on channel 26. (New London's WTWS, the only station that came in clear on the TV in Carter's room.) You took to palling around with my closest female friend, Amy—you and she making a regular team in games of Spades, voicing a united feminist front, as you were often the only two girls in a big group of guys. The time when you two convinced me, after hours of bullshitting argument, that I really should say that Todd threw like "someone who hadn't grown up throwing a baseball" instead of "a girl," I warmed with that particular sense of matchmaker's validation—you saw what I saw in them; they saw what I saw in you.

It had worked, I marveled. Problem solved. Girlfriend imported. World rescued from the brink, remade any way we wanted it. I felt like a wizard. And at the age of nineteen, a champion.

It wasn't so awesome for so long, though. And maybe it was never actually as awesome for anybody else as it was for me. Understandably, you had some qualms about your role as the imported girlfriend. It was a compromised position from the outset, all of your friends having been my friends first. And your status at the school was officially uncertain; we didn't know where you'd be the next year. And there were other problems—deeper ones, in hindsight—probably best explainable, or at least most broadly explainable, as you growing up and out of love with me. For whatever reason or reasons, halfway through the semester, you were rarely in anything other than a bad mood, and we were having sex far less frequently than I wanted us to be.

And then you went to Vermont for the weekend with your parents, and I cheated on you with Amy.

I confessed that Sunday night, after you'd returned, but before we went to sleep. We were lying in bed, our heads on our pillows. "I have something to tell you," I said, and I told you. You sat up and looked at me, and the expression on your face melted into one that I had never seen before and that I don't like to think about even today.

"Did you fuck her?" you asked; your eyes were wet and red and wider at the bottom like bells. I hadn't. But it didn't matter.

I slept on Carter's couch that night, my original roommates having moved my bed out of the room, and every night for the next week. It was a horrible week. I brought you food from the cafeteria downstairs because you didn't want to see anybody. You sat on the bed with a pile of crumpled-up tissues. I came to understand what a great song Wham!'s "Careless Whisper" is, George Michael singing about how guilty feet have got no rhythm. I'd never liked it before.

You took me back eventually. An act of grace likely attributable to the fact that you didn't really know anyone else in the state of Connecticut. Cutting you off from Amy as I had was perhaps the worst part of the whole thing. Who could you talk to about it? Even once you were feeling okay enough to sleep in the same bed with me, though, you told me that you didn't think you would ever be able to forgive me, not entirely.

"Really?" I said. "Never?"

"I don't think so," you said.

But you were calm when you said it and not angry, and I figured the feeling would eventually pass. We lived in that room together—where we left our clothes on the floor and listened to Michelle Shocked's "Anchorage" over and over again and rested our feet on each other's when we read—and I was convinced that we would be like that, together, until the day one of us died. I couldn't imagine any other scenario. I pictured us older, living in a house, sitting in the kitchen or cooking dinner or whatever. You holding a grudge because I touched someone else's boob when we were teenagers? That didn't seem like how it would be.

We survived the next couple months, and I thought things were getting better. But it was hard to know because I was such a drunken mess all the time. At the end of the semester, after we'd finished our classes and taken our finals, you'd spent our last night at school in our room, packing for home. I'd chosen to spend it drinking Milwaukee's Best and Southern Comfort and jumping up and down on furniture while screaming along to Replacements songs with Carter and Matt and Will and Steve and Drew and Todd until we were all blind and hugging and telling each other how much we were going to miss each other. And so was lying in bed the next day, unable to function while you and my mom put all my stuff in bags and boxes and brought it out to the car. And so was unable to figure out how to get all the letters you'd written me into a bag when I found them in the drawer of my bureau on a final sweep through my original dorm room. And so just left them there and limped downstairs.

That summer was not a good one for us. What had long been a playful needle-and-nag dynamic had calcified into something less healthy. You were too often honestly disappointed in me; I was too often giving you wholly legitimate reasons for being so. You would register complaint; I would parry with jokes rather than any real effort toward remedy— reveling, or wallowing, in what I took to be my role as the lovable fuckup. Even after most of the lovable part had worn off. Looking back, I think we hung on to each other more out of stasis and fear than anything else. Fear of the change, of what the world would be like on our own, of what it would mean to finally leave high school and our hometown and the comfort of things we'd known as kids. Things we should have been ready to leave behind earlier but were not.

It was when you heard about the letters, I think, that you started the long process of ending it. We'd been home from Connecticut for a month or so when I told you. We were at our old grade school, Markham Place, where we had first met, in seventh grade, when your family moved to our town. I don't know what we were doing there. Just hanging out, I suppose, sitting on one of the benches up at the top of the hill, looking down at the baseball field and the gazebo and the library. I don't know why I told you, whether you asked where they were or if it had just come up in conversation. I mentioned it casually, that I'd left them in that drawer at college. I didn't think it was any big deal, and I was surprised when you got as angry as you did. I thought you were kidding at first. But you were not. You were aghast. "I can't believe you," you said. "I've kept every letter you've ever written me!"

I didn't understand. We saw each other every day. And like I said, I was confident in the belief that we would be together for the rest of our lives. I figured you could just tell me what was in the letters if you wanted me to know.

I was missing a larger point. You shook your head and let out a little laugh. A sad, disgusted cough of a laugh. But at yourself, not at me. You told me that you thought you knew me better than you apparently did. You told me, for the first time, that the thought had occurred to you that we should break up.

"I deserve better," you said. "I deserve someone who keeps the letters I write."

You were right. Letters are important. There's a difference between saying something out loud and putting it down in writing. Writing is more effortful, more carefully thought out, and in that way, more intimate. Letters are less ephemeral (obviously) and so serve well as a time capsule. And as a looking glass into a person's mind state. Beyond the words themselves even, you can tell a lot from the slant of someone's handwriting or the flow of the script. So handwritten letters are especially special.

I recently found an old letter of yours actually. (I made sure to keep every one you sent after that conversation.) You wrote me a to-do list: some errands I needed to take care of, some things I needed for "life improvement." Last on the list, though, was a joke referencing an argument we had gotten into that stemmed from something that had happened one day when we were playing Spades. We had been partners in this game, you and I, and I had made a reckless play, endangering our team's fortunes for the thrill of taking a risk.

"Regret dismissing my bid," you wrote, "and sacrificing the team's score for personal enjoyment for a long, long, long time. Say, fifty years?"

It's funny. But I know there were some serious feelings behind the joke. It's been twenty-two years so far. You were always a very good letter writer.

■ ■ ■

Dear Drivers of Cars Driving onto the Gooseneck Bridge in Oceanport, New Jersey, That Day at the End of the Summer of 1990,

Sorry my father and I almost killed you with a runaway boat.

It had been a hard summer. My father's cancer continued to progress. He'd had it for a year and four months already, which was great in some ways because that was a year and two months longer than the doctors had told him he had to live when he was diagnosed. But while he was up and about most of the time, the disease had taken a toll. He looked different, like a shrunken version of himself. And smelled different—these big pills he was taking, prescribed by some alternative healing guru, large, clear yellow capsules filled with a liquid that looked even yellower, they gave his skin a sickly, acrid odor. His voice was softer. Most disturbing, to him at least, was that the tumors in his brain were beginning to show effects.

That day he had asked me to help him bring our boat, a twenty-six-foot cabin cruiser, from our driveway, where it had sat since we'd taken it out of the water a week or so before, to the boatyard in Neptune where it stayed covered in tarp for the winter. We went out through the carport and each took a side of the large triangular trailer. We lifted it a few inches off the gravel and swung it into position behind the car, lining up the front point, which rolled on a smaller wheel than the two in the back, with the doorknob-shaped hitch attached just below the license plate. He asked me if I could lock it in place. I didn't know how, I said, though I had watched him do this twice a year since I was a kid.

He shook his head and *tsk*ed.

"Come on, Dave," he said. "You're eighteen years old. You drive a car. You don't know how to put a trailer on a hitch? You've got to learn this stuff."

It was in this particular area that I was, and am, most different from my father. He was a tougher, outdoorsy, can-do type. He liked to go camping and skiing, and he kept a shed next to our house with a Peg-Board wall hung with tools. He would bring me out there when I was little and let me crank the vise tight while he worked on small carpentry projects or did some minor auto repair. But I never learned the difference between a wrench and a ratchet. I never learned how to pitch a tent or not lose my mind because of mosquitoes—and while I liked skiing, too, I always had to go in early because my toes got too cold.

"I'll do it," he said unhappily. "You lift."

I hoisted the trailer onto the hitch and watched—halfway, still not getting it—as he knelt down and did whatever latching or bolting things he did to lock them together. (I would never learn how to do anything like this. I tried to change a lightbulb last week and ended up unscrewing part of the fixture. It's sitting on a shelf as I type.)

When we were done, I offered to drive and held my hand out for the keys. He said no. If he had to be in charge, he'd be in charge.

So he drove and I rode shotgun and tried not to think about how he smelled, or how lately, a wincing gasp would interrupt a family dinner, a sharp cry might come from his room late at night. He'd recently told me that it sometimes felt like his brain was trying to crack out of his skull. A couple weeks before, we had watched a movie together, and when I'd brought it up the next day, he couldn't remember anything about it. He reached up and held his head in both hands and said, "I can't even fucking think anymore!"

That day that we almost killed you, though, he seemed fine. We'd only been driving for a couple of minutes. The

Gooseneck Bridge was near our house, connecting our town, Little Silver, to Oceanport across the Shrewsbury River. We had just passed the highest point on the bridge and were on the downhill slope when I heard a noise from the back of the car. I turned to look and saw the boat swinging away from us into the other lane. There are only two lanes on the Gooseneck Bridge.

"Dad!" I said. "The boat!"

He turned to look and saw what had happened, that the trailer had come unhitched. "Holy shit!"

He leaned on the horn and swerved the car back and forth like he couldn't decide whether or not he should try to get in the boat's way. But in a second it was passing us in the oncoming traffic lane.

I sat stunned as we saw you, two cars approaching the bridge on the Oceanport side. My father blared the horn some more and unrolled his window and started waving his arm. "Get off the road," he shouted. But you couldn't hear him.

You saw, though, and slowed, thank god, and pulled over by the reeds as our boat hit the curb and careened back into our lane in front of us. It rolled downhill like that, gaining speed and passing you—your wide-open mouths and eyes—on its way to rumbling off the road and crashing into a chain-link fence at the base of the bridge.

We pulled up behind it and stopped the car, and my father exhaled. "Jesus Christ," he said. "We could have killed someone."

He tried to motion you a mea culpa, but you drove off up over the bridge. You would have a good story to tell.

"I don't know what happened," my father said, looking at the steering wheel. "I could have sworn it was latched. I could have sworn I checked it."

We got out to survey the damage. The trailer was banged up, but only a little bit, the one small wheel at the front knocked out of alignment. A couple of the posts of the fence had come up out of the ground, but otherwise it was fine—the chain-link mesh had given like a net. The boat looked okay, too, still strapped in its place.

None of this mattered to my father. He was shaking his head and had a self-questioning expression on his face I didn't recognize. "I don't know what happened," he said again, aloud, but not really to me. "I always check it. I always double-check it."

The Oceanport Police Department was visible from where we were standing. A low, flat brick building on the corner of Monmouth Boulevard and the road the bridge turns into, Myrtle Avenue. Within a couple of minutes, we watched a police car pull out of the parking lot, flash its roof lights, and slowly drive over to us. It parked on the grass by our boat, its door opened, and an officer stepped out. He frowned at the boat and the trailer and the fence before turning to us.

"Who was driving?" he said.

"I was," my father said. "I don't know what happened, Officer, I..."

The police officer cut him off. "This was an extremely dangerous situation."

"I know," my father said. "It could have killed somebody. *I could have* killed somebody. I'm lucky I didn't kill somebody."

My father explained what had happened, how he usually checked the latch so carefully, how it was a point of pride for him. The police officer was gruff, and eyed him accusingly, and mentioned the possibility of arrest and charges of reckless endangerment. And when my father finally copped to the truth, when he admitted that he had cancer and in his brain and that it was affecting his thinking, that was the worst part of the whole day, the worst part of that whole summer, the sound of my dad's voice when he said that. How clear it was that he didn't want to be saying it.

The cop took my dad's identification and told him he'd have to pay to repair the fence. But then he let us go.

He said that I should drive, though. So I did. Like I should have driven there to begin with. Like I should have been able to hitch the trailer to our car and make sure the latch was closed tight, safe, secure.

■ ■ ■

Dear Dad,

Sorry I didn't come right away when you called me.

This happened on December 25, 1990, the day you died.

Since you are dead now, and I don't imagine that you can read this, or hear it, or know my thoughts or anything, I suppose this is more of an apology to myself. For screwing up in a way that has made me feel bad since. Not horribly, terribly bad—I don't beat myself up over it too much. But it's one of those things that I wish I could do over again. I would do it differently.

We were on an airplane, returning from Rochester, New York, where we'd just celebrated the holiday with Mom's family, home to New Jersey. You, Mom, Debby, and me. I don't know why we chose to fly on Christmas Day. Do you get cheaper tickets on Christmas?

You were sick, sicker than you'd been since the initial chemotherapy treatment a year and a half earlier. You'd outlived the doctors' original prognosis by sixteen months, doing better at some times than at others, but had recently taken a deep downturn. We had just gotten you a wheelchair because your feet had swollen up to the point where it hurt to walk on them. I remember the expression on Uncle Tom's face as he pushed you out the door when the cab had come. His effort to smile when we said good-bye.

On the plane, soon after the pilot switched off the fasten your seat belts signs, you said you had to go to the bathroom. The wheelchair had been stowed in the luggage hold; we'd boarded the plane early, you walking tenderly, with help from Mom and me. So I got up with you, and stood behind you, and held you by your elbows, supporting your weight as we moved down the aisle. You were light, your bones felt thin.

But with people sitting in the other seats now, it was a more difficult trip than I'd expected. The flight was surprisingly full for Christmas Day. I glanced down and saw the purple wool booties a friend of yours had knit to cover your socks. They were stretched out like each one had a Nerf football inside it, dragging as much as walking. I felt the other passengers looking at us and I felt embarrassed. I looked straight ahead, avoiding their eyes. Then I felt ashamed for feeling embarrassed. What, was I going to pick up a girl? I kicked one of your feet. You winced and told me to be careful.

When we got to the bathroom, I helped you inside and you grabbed the handrail tight. We decided we'd leave the door unlocked, so I could get back in if you needed more help. "Stand right outside," you said. "So you can hear if I call, okay?" Your voice was raspy.

I said I would, and I closed the door and stepped into a space around a corner, in front of the first row of seats nearby, but out of the aisle so people could pass if they needed to. Crouching slightly, I looked up at the cabin ceiling. I didn't want to look out over the other passengers. I didn't want to see what I thought might be pity in their eyes.

I heard two people having a conversation in a language I didn't recognize. I tilted my head toward their voices, trying to figure out what country they might be from. (I'm always interested in that sort of thing.) They went on for a bit and I couldn't get it. Were they speaking Greek? Turkish? Romanian? Is Romanian a language?

I was still straining to hear them when I heard your voice,

faint but urgent, calling my name. I realized right away that I had in fact heard you a couple times already—but not registered it immediately because I was concentrating on the foreign language. I rushed to the door, and you called again as I pushed it open and saw you on the floor next to the toilet. Your pants and underwear were down, and your pale, gaunt legs were folded awkwardly beneath you. You looked up at me. Your eyes were scared.

"I was calling you!"

I stood and blinked for a second, hot with chagrin. I felt like a little boy who had just broken something important.

"I fell," you said.

I snapped to and leaned down and grabbed you under your arms. "Here," I said. "Let me get you up."

I lifted you up and sat you on the toilet, holding you there with my hands. You were breathing heavily, and your face didn't look like itself.

"Are you all right?" I said.

"I don't know," you said.

We waited for a moment, and then your mouth curled downward on one side. Your eyes clouded and closed. You made a sound like "*eeaughh*" and your head lolled forward.

I pulled you closer and kept you upright, letting your head rest on my shoulder. I didn't know what to do. You'd been having episodic loss of consciousness over the past few months, Mom had told me. Like mini-seizures, the doctors said they were. So I waited for you to wake up. After a few minutes, though, once I felt your drool soak through my shirt, I called out for help. No one heard at first, so I kicked the door and shouted louder. "Help!"

A man came to the door and then Mom a moment later. She squeezed in next to me and helped me hold you. I told her what had happened, and she guessed it was another mini-seizure. I heard the pilot come over the address system and ask if there were any medical professionals on board. I had never been on a plane or in a restaurant or any other place when that call had gone out: "Is there a doctor in the house?" It seemed like something from TV. I had the strangely dissociative realization that he was talking about us, our family; we were the emergency. Like we were the people on TV.

Mom and I sat there with you, crouched down in front of you, taking turns supporting your weight, waiting for you to wake up. For a long time; must have been ten minutes. While she was holding you, I stared at your lips and nostrils to see if I could see any tiny movement. I don't know at what point exactly I had started to wonder if you were dead. But I was wondering. I wished I had a hand mirror. After a while, a quiet while, I could tell from her face that Mom was wondering the same thing.

"Do you think…," I said.

"I don't know," Mom said.

"I can't tell if he's breathing."

"Neither can I," she said.

I put my fingers on your throat, on your Adam's apple. I thought I felt a pulse, but I didn't trust myself to distinguish between your pulse and the pulse in my fingertips. I didn't know whether I was putting my fingers in the right place.

"I don't know," I said.

Eventually a pilot came with a man who was, I think, not a doctor but a pharmacist or dentist, and we pulled up your pants and they pulled you out of the bathroom and set you in a chair across the aisle. They put a blanket over you, and Mom sat next to you with her arm around you. An ambulance had been called to meet the plane when it landed, they said. I went back to go sit with Debby, who was only twelve, and a flight attendant in a billowy blouse who had been sitting with her. Debby was crying and asked me what was going on, and I told her I wasn't sure. That you fell and lost consciousness and that there'd be a doctor meeting the plane when it landed. The flight attendant started crying, too, and told us that her father had died just last year. I guess everyone was fairly certain what had happened, that you had died—I bet the pharmacist knew how to check for a pulse; I imagine him shaking his head to the pilot, quickly, secretly, so Mom couldn't see—but no one being a doctor, no one was going to make the final call. I don't blame them. You wouldn't want to be wrong about something like that.

I pretty much knew it. I was strangely calm, though. I felt cool and numb and far away from everything. Like I was somewhere way deep down inside myself, looking out at my hands and my clothes and Debby and the flight attendant, this stranger, crying next to me, as if it were all through a window, or a telescope, or the periscope of a submarine.

An hour later, we were in a brick-walled, warehouse-like security station at the Newark airport. The ambulance had driven right up on the runway—I saw the flashing red lights as we landed—and EMT guys had boarded the plane and put you on a stretcher and carried you off. That part was fast and chaotic. Mom told them, with more volume and urgency than she usually spoke with, that you did not want to be resuscitated or kept alive on a respirator—that you'd signed a directive saying so. She and Debby and I had been taken to the station to wait. A man came in and called Mom into another room, and when she returned, she smiled at us with tears in her eyes and opened her arms and said, "Oh, kids!" and we all hugged. Deb started bawling and Mom said, "We're going to be okay."

The strange farawayness I felt on the plane lasted for days. As relatives arrived, and old family friends, and more food and cards and flowers than we knew what to do with. As I told the rabbi that I did not want to speak at the funeral because I didn't have anything to say—I didn't, not in public, not then. As I sat in the front pew, while Ava, your sister, clutched the podium and swayed through her eulogy and David Landy told warm, funny stories about you. As we drove to the cemetery and stood in front of all those people and threw dirt on your casket and the clatter of pebbles and stones on the cold wood planks sounded appropriately real and physical and final to me. As the bright green Astroturf they laid over the top when we were done looked the opposite. As Thea and Pa, your parents from Germany, broke down when the rabbi started his prayer—"Gerht, we sing Kaddish for our Peter!" And sobs and sobs and white knuckles clutching winter coats. "I know! I know!"

I was right there for all of this. And very conscious of how I was holding my face. I smiled a lot but tried not to show my teeth, so as not to appear goofy or joyous. I wanted to support everyone who was so sad and emotional. And I remember thinking, as I looked out at the swirl all around, *This is what it feels like when your father dies.* But I didn't really have a good gauge on it.

Sometime around that time, the day after the funeral, or two days after, I was upstairs in your room with Mom. She was on the phone. I was emptying the drawers of your bureau, going through your stuff, deciding which socks I would take, which belts, should I use your old wallet?

"Yes," Mom was saying to somebody. "We're sad. But we're okay. We think it was a good death. A blood vessel burst in his brain. The doctor said it would have happened quickly, and he wouldn't have felt any pain. And David was there with him. He would have wanted that."

Listening to her, I thought of myself on the plane, standing outside the bathroom, looking up at the ceiling, listening to the voices I was trying to figure out. I thought of the moment I realized that the other sound I was hearing, the faint, recurring, plaintive sound, was you calling for help. And those two seconds of delay, and the fear on your face when I finally opened the door.

I still think about it.

■ ■ ■

Dear Winnie Loeffler,

I'm sorry for making you feel uncomfortable.

This was January 1991. You were in a good mood, perhaps because you were to be graduating that spring. We had just returned from winter break. We hadn't seen each other in almost a month when I bumped into you on the second floor of the library. We hugged hello. Then you got that look like you'd just remembered something. "Dave," you said. "I didn't know your dad made pens."

I gulped. This was not a conversation that would end well. "Umm...pens?" I said.

You then pulled a pen out of your pocket and held it up for me to see. It was one of those click-button pens with the clear plastic top with liquid in it. The type you find at a gift shop at a tourist spot, with a skier skiing down a mountain or a sliding San Francisco trolley car. In this one, though, there was a small man dressed in a blue suit. You turned it upside down and the suit fell away, revealing his large erection.

"That's him, right?" You giggled devilishly, readying your zinger. "You must be so proud!"

I laughed, too. This was a funny joke. Of a kind we'd often enjoyed together. I've always liked dirty jokes. Especially ones about friends' family members or, in turn, my own family members. The fun of being good humored about topics that make other people uncomfortable, I guess.

But now there was a problem. I didn't know what to do. I didn't want to make you uncomfortable. You were my friend, whom I liked to laugh with so much, who was also good humored about topics that made other people uncomfortable.

You were about to be uncomfortable, though. I knew this. Part of me thought that I shouldn't say anything. But I knew you'd find out soon; you'd talk to Carter or Todd or someone else who knew. Someone would tell you and you'd feel bad then, probably even worse. I thought we might as well get it over with.

"Umm, Winnie?" I started. "I don't want you to feel bad about this. It's really okay. And I'm sorry this is happening this way. But I guess you should know: my dad just died."

Your face fell. You went white. You knew I wasn't kidding. Then your cheeks blushed bright and you giggled. But not in the nice devilish way this time. You covered your mouth.

"I mean not *just* just," I said. "Like three weeks ago. It's okay." He'd had cancer for a year and a half. It's likely that you didn't even know that. I didn't talk about it a lot.

"Oh my god," you said. Your eyes were wide.

"I'm sorry," I said, trying to sound as okay about it as I could. "I would have told you. We hadn't seen each other. I didn't mean to tell you like this."

"I...am...so...sorry..."

"It's really okay."

It really was. Your joke didn't make me feel bad. It's not

like you telling me that the guy with the big dick in the pen was my father *reminded* me that my father had died. Like I hadn't been thinking about it up to that point.

In fact, just the night before, some guys in my dorm had rented *Lethal Weapon 2* and put it on the TV in the living room. There were a bunch of us watching, like twenty people, and it came to the part where Mel Gibson has to save Danny Glover, who is trapped in his bathroom, sitting on his toilet because he has discovered that the Afrikaner bad guys have rigged it with a bomb that will explode if he stands up.

Danny Glover is scared and says to Mel Gibson, "I'm gonna die on the toilet."

"Guys like you don't die on toilets," Mel Gibson says.

And I thought about what that meant, by implication, about my father, who was a guy, it just so happened, who had died on a toilet.

I got up off the couch without saying anything to anyone and went upstairs and lay down in my bed. It actually hadn't bothered me, watching that scene. At least, not in the way that I thought it might have. I didn't catch my breath or feel a stab of pain in my heart. I had seen the movie before, so I'd known it was coming. And I knew it was just a stupid Mel Gibson movie anyway (stupid but very exciting and funny and with one of the all-time great endings when the racist South African villain says, "Diplomatic immunity," and Danny Glover shoots him and says, "It's just been revoked!") And what did that have to do with real life? Except, yes, reaffirm that there are certain circumstances under which people die that seem less dignified to society at large than other circumstances might. But I knew that already, and it didn't much matter to me.

Mostly I went upstairs because it struck me that I *should* be feeling upset upon seeing such a scene in a movie three weeks after my father died. And the fact that I was not feeling upset, but was only *thinking* about how, on paper, in the abstract, someone in my situation *might* feel upset—well, that's what made me feel bad. Or not even bad, but just extra introspective and like I didn't want to be sitting in a living room with a bunch of guys watching *Lethal Weapon 2* anymore.

Honestly, if anything, your joke made me feel better. It was good to be back at school. Back with friends. Away from home, where the credenza in the kitchen was covered with condolence cards and the fridge was filled with whitefish. (I love whitefish. But Jesus, you can only eat so much of the stuff.) It was good to be subject to the dirty jokes, the teasing, the bullshit back and forth that marks normal life. In fact, as much as I felt bad that you had to learn the news in such an unfortunate way, a devilish part of me was glad.

Talk about a zinger.

■ ■ ■

Dear Riders of the Powell-Mason Cable Car Line in San Francisco,

Sorry for flashing you.

I was living at 1612 Mason Street that summer, in 1991, in an apartment on the bottom floor of a gray-and-purple building at the corner of Green Street in North Beach. A particularly picturesque San Francisco spot. Pine trees rose above Russian Hill a steep block to the west. There was a view from the roof out over Grace Cathedral and Fisherman's Wharf to Alcatraz in the bay. Cable cars ran right past our front door.

The only way I was able to afford such a nice place was to share its two bedrooms with four friends from college. I'd been asked to take what a kindly dean referred to as an "academic hiatus" after a sophomore year that had ended with my grade-point average somewhere around one-point-four. I thought I'd get a job and start a new life. But that was a recession summer. Jobs were not to be found. I ate tuna fish sandwiches and potato salad every day, saving every spare bit of cash for rent and the amazing pot a friend of a friend brought us down from Humboldt County every week. The only furniture in the apartment was a kitchen table and chairs. We slept on futon cushions and didn't much decorate.

Or hang curtains on the windows in my bedroom. Those windows looked out onto Mason Street, down the middle of which, every half hour or so, a red-and-yellow trolley full of tourists would slowly clatter and chug its way toward the intersection. My roommates and I joked about being a sight-seeing attraction and living in a fishbowl and carried our clothes into the bathroom to change after showering. But as the months passed and I got more comfortable in the apartment, I started walking back into the room in a towel and changing there. You could hear the cable cars approaching from a block away, so there was always time to cover up. Eventually, though, due in part to the listlessness of unemployment, in part to the Ginsberg and Bukowski poems I was spending a lot of time reading in the reading room at the City Lights bookstore a few blocks away, I stopped making the effort. What did I care if a couple tourists saw me naked? Consider it an extra perk or a hidden tax that accompanies the price of a ticket. Either way, a different kind of San Francisco treat.

This was early in the handheld video camera era. I was struck by the number of people who rode the cable cars with these things fixed to one eye, making such effort to keep them steady, filming the façade of every building on the route. I always thought they were missing a lot that way, sacrificing 360-degree scenery for dull documentation. Didn't they want to look around? It didn't seem like a fun way to spend a vacation day. Perhaps for this reason and perhaps because of the potency of the Humboldt pot, I got a real kick out of it the first time I saw a guy's face pop out from behind his camera, eyes and mouth open wide, having spotted the whole of me through his lens. That'd give him a story to tell. Spice things up a bit. Soon I took to air-drying after a shower, staying naked on purpose, waiting to hear the trolley come and standing right up in the window, hands on my hips, giggling stoned to myself as it passed. It was rare that anyone noticed—only two or three gawkers and pointers over a month or so of this—but I very much enjoyed the thought of the people who might have caught me on camera without noticing in real time. That would be a fun home movie screening. Greetings from San Francisco!

But if you didn't find it fun, well, sorry. Also, please keep in mind what Mark Twain said about how cold it is in San Francisco during the summer.

■ ■ ■

Dear Bob Mould,

I'm sorry for ruining your solo acoustic concert.

It was fall 1991. You were playing the Fast Lane in Asbury Park, New Jersey, near where I grew up. And near where I was living then. I had failed out of college the previous semester and gone out to San Francisco, but I was unable to find a job and so had to move back home with my mom and my little sister.

I was and still am a huge fan of your music—that which you made with Hüsker Dü in the '80s and the solo albums you'd released more recently. At school, before I left, my

friends and I listened to you all the time. It was pained, angry music, and we were a pained and angry bunch. Though I doubt we would have copped to that description at the time. We wore ripped jeans and baseball caps and drank too much and issued the kind of unrelenting stream of obnoxious banter that tries a bit too hard to prove it doesn't care about anything.

We'd seen you play the year before at Toad's Place in New Haven—a blaring, stomping, glorious performance with the new band you'd assembled that left our ears ringing and our minds blown. So when I heard you were coming to the Fast Lane, I called Will and Carter to see if they'd want to take the train down. They did. I got tickets.

The day of the show, I picked them up at the station with beers in the car. I was psyched for a big night. I was realizing around that time how much more I liked being at college with my friends than at home with my mom and little sister. We drank through dinner like we were making up for lost time.

The club was crowded when we got there. We went straight to the bar and bought as many double vodkas and Long Island iced teas as we could carry before pushing our way to a spot at the front of the stage, which was the perfect height to rest our drinks on. We'd each smuggled in a couple airplane bottles for refills, and we lined them up there, too. We screamed with laughter as we waited for you to come on. We were surely the loudest people there, getting rowdy, throwing each other elbows. We were ready to rock.

Needless to say, we were taken aback when you walked onto the stage alone, holding an acoustic guitar, and sat down on a stool. We were far too drunk to stand still and watch anything quiet and intimate. We wanted to slam dance.

"Fuck that!" Carter yelled while the rest of the audience clapped and cheered. "What is this, Jim Croce? Plug that thing in, Bob! We wanna fuckin' rock!"

Of course, you aren't Jim Croce. You started with "Wishing Well," a favorite of ours, and you strummed hard. So we got into it and proceeded to have a great time. Unfortunately for you and everyone else in attendance that night, we did this by basically pretending we were at the full-band, full-throttle electric rock show we'd come hoping to see. We whooped and hollered and screamed along with the lyrics. We continued to demand more and louder rocking. We jostled each other back and forth, knocking our glasses and bottles over, and eventually started something to the effect of a three-man mosh pit. This while you were sitting down. This much to the dismay of those audience members in our vicinity who were, in fact, trying to stand still and watch something quiet and intimate.

People were clearly and expressively unhappy with our behavior. We ignored them. At one point, you flicked a still-lit cigarette butt at us, hitting me in the shoulder. (A nice shot. Must have been fifteen feet.) Carter took off my baseball cap and threw it up onto the stage. But throughout the evening, despite the cigarette butt, despite the frown on your face,

I imagined you as somehow approving of our shenanigans. (The cigarette butt could've just been joining in on our fun. And back then, you always had a frown on your face.) You must appreciate our enthusiasm, I thought, the fact that we knew all the words to your songs. And how proud of us you must be, for flying the loud fast punk rock flag, even at a solo acoustic show. Or at least, how proud you *ought* to be.

I was mistaken. You glared at us after finishing your last song, "Whichever Way the Wind Blows," and violently unstrapped your guitar. When you bent down to pick up my hat, I thought you were going to toss it back to me. I held out my hands and got ready to thank you. You held it up for a moment so I could get a good look at it, then threw it as far as you could out into the crowd at the back of the room. Then you flipped me the bird and stomped your combat boots right offstage. Now *that's* punk rock!

Of course, as I've grown older, I feel less and less like there was anything to be proud of in the way I acted at that concert. The music, from what I remember of it, was awesome. Quiet and intimate but still powerful and pained and angry. And I don't like the thought that, even for one stupid night during a troubled time of my life, you were pained by *me*, angry at *me*.

I'm different than that now.

■ ■ ■

Dear Derek,

Sorry for stinking.

You were seven years old at the time, which was December 19, 1991. I remember because I had just turned twenty-one. The day before, as a matter of fact. You were in the first grade at a school for emotionally disturbed children in New Jersey, where I worked as an assistant to your teacher, Suzanne.

You had been having a hard enough year already. Your mother had died. She'd been murdered, Suzanne had told me, and—and this is beyond anything I can imagine—you saw it happen. You were living with your mom's family, your grandmother and your uncles. But it was not an optimal situation. There were drug and alcohol problems in the household apparently. You had been removed from your local mainstream school because you'd been having trouble controlling your anger. You'd been lashing out physically, and it had become a safety issue. Much of my job for the first couple of months you were in Suzanne's class consisted of sitting with you on the linoleum floor, holding you in the official restraint position I'd been taught—your arms wrapped across your chest in an X, each of your legs pinned under one of my own—as you screamed and thrashed against me. You hit me and kicked me plenty of times. It never hurt too badly. You threw a chair at me once, which hurt a little more. But still, you were just seven.

And a really lovely kid besides. You were smart and warm and wiseacre funny, and we spent a lot of calmer time talking.

My father had died that year. And one of the reasons Suzanne assigned me to you directly, she said, was because you were able to open up to me.

We were sitting at your desk once, working in your math workbook, when you got quiet and turned to me and asked me if I had pictures of my father at my house. I said yes, I did. Your family had recently put away all the pictures of your mother; seeing them had been making you too upset.

"I don't even remember what she looks like," you said, and you held your head in your hands and started to cry in a different way than how kids usually cry.

In many respects, that job at the school is the hardest I've ever worked. It wasn't long hours, 8:30 a.m. to 2:30 p.m. But though I usually drank four or five cups of coffee in that span every day, as soon as I got home, I'd fall into my bed and sleep for the rest of the afternoon. In hindsight, I guess I might have been suffering a touch of depression. As much as I liked you and the other kids in the class, as rewarding as I found the job, my life was not the way I wanted it to be. I was living with my mom and my sister, getting used to the house without my father in it. My mom had turned my old bedroom into her office, so I was sleeping downstairs on a convertible couch we left open, in what had been a waiting room for my dad's clients—he was a psychologist with a home-based private practice. The moss-green carpeting in there was left over from the '70s, and it made a squishy sound when you stepped on it. Most of my friends from high school were away at their colleges. I was taking night classes at Brookdale Community College and spending a lot of time alone.

I decided I had to get out of there. So I made sure I got good grades at Brookdale and sent my transcripts up to my original college's deans' office as soon as I'd earned enough make-up credits. By mid-December, when people were arriving home for Christmas break, I had already started preparing for my return to Connecticut, but I was nonetheless eager to socialize. The night of my twenty-first birthday, my friend Mark, who had turned twenty-one in August, took me out for my first legal drink in a bar. We went to Brannigan's, an Irish pub down by Marine Park in Red Bank. It was a Thursday night, and we chose Brannigan's because we figured it would be less crowded than the more popular Globe Hotel across the street. But there were still lots of beefy guys in goatees and overcoats. We were still in New Jersey in the early '90s. (You've seen Kevin Smith's movies, right?)

My first legal drink turned into a great many legal drinks, of course. With various strangers and acquaintances buying me birthday shots. Much of the night is a blur in my memory. The way it ended, though, is all too clear. Two guys I knew from high school, Karl and Rob, they'd graduated a couple years before Mark and I and were drinking down at the far end of the bar. They never liked me and my friends much, I don't think. Karl knew karate, we'd learned one night a few years before, when he'd choked my buddy Dave almost to death during a fight at a party over a girl. (It was scary. Dave lost consciousness; all these blood vessels in his eyes burst. He looked like a Halloween mask for weeks.) And Rob, who had worked delivering pizzas for the same pizza place that I did, had warned me, on my first day on the job, not to accept offers of sex from any of my delivery customers. "Trust me," he said, "don't go inside. There's gonna be some big dude in there waiting to jump out and beat the shit out of you." All right, I told him, not at all expecting this to ever happen. "Don't get me wrong," he went on. "I've banged my share of customers—we all have. But you gotta be careful." I never knew quite what to make of that. He was not the type of guy you would ever believe had had sex with pizza delivery customers. But then, I don't know.

Anyway, the night at Brannigan's, when I had already had far too much to drink, Karl and Rob called me over to say they wanted to buy me a shot. "A Cement Mixer," Rob said. His smile was a sneer. I should have been leery, but I was too drunk to care.

A warning: If anyone ever offers to buy you a Cement Mixer, do not accept. It is not a real shot. As it turns out, a Cement Mixer is a mix of Baileys Irish Cream and lime juice. The lime juice curdles the cream, turning it to a consistency not unlike that of wet cement. I vomited soon after gulping it down. Right on the bar, which made the bartender very angry. (Though it was as much his fault as anyone's for serving such a drunk person such a not funny "gag" drink in the first place.) He demanded that I leave, and Mark ended up in a shouting match with him that almost turned into a fistfight, and we were both eventually removed from the premises by force. And thus, ridiculously, I found myself officially banned for life from the establishment that had served me my first legal alcoholic drink.

So it was not my best birthday. I should have called in sick to work the next day. But I was still pretty drunk when I woke up and didn't realize how bad my hangover would get. Also, I wouldn't have wanted to let Suzanne down, or you, or any of the other kids in the class.

By around ten thirty or so that morning, it was clear I'd made a mistake. The class was in its gym period, and I was lying with my face against the cool, rubberized floor. You were supposed to be playing kickball or Red Light, Green Light or something, but were instead leaning on me and talking to me—at me mostly; I wasn't doing a very good job of talking back. My head was ringing with pain, and my skin felt clammy underneath my clothes.

"What's wrong?" you asked me.

"I don't feel very good today," I said, trying to breathe as slowly as I could.

You sniffed the air and said, "You stink!"

"Thanks," I said.

"You smell like whiskey," you said.

I had been feeling bad about the fact that I was planning to leave to go back up to college for the next semester. I don't remember whether I'd told you yet or not. Right then, though, as I was beginning to realize the limits of the tragicomic wastrel persona I had been cultivating for years. ("It's just not that cute anymore," Bill Murray's girlfriend told him, breaking up with him at the beginning of *Stripes*. "It's a *little* cute," Bill Murray retorted, in a line that I'd long embraced like a daily affirmation.) Right then, considering that and the various elements of your situation at home and at school, I had the thought that you might be better off without me. Not that that made me feel any less guilty.

I knew I stunk.

■ ■ ■

Dear President Clinton,

I'm sorry I wrote that thing about you getting caught with underage girls on the bulletin board at Bob Kerrey's campaign headquarters during the New Hampshire primary in 1992.

Truth is, I had no business being in anyone's campaign headquarters at that point in my life. I had recently returned to college from hiatus, but not for the right reasons. I was not at all politically active or even very politically interested. My friend Matt, though, had been volunteering for Kerrey that winter and dragged a carload of us up from our Connecticut campus to pitch in for the final weekend before the vote. Poor judgment on his part.

While Matt was assigned to more important jobs, or perhaps just ones that required a more presentable demeanor, Will, Todd, Carter, and I made cold calls from the phone bank in the dreary Manchester office, hiding warm cans of Milwaukee's Best between our legs and sneaking outside every few minutes to smoke bowls by a Dumpster in the parking lot. (Jesus, those cold calls. "Hi! Do you have a minute? I'd like to talk to you about why I'm supporting Bob Kerrey for president." That's like a hundred more people I should be apologizing to. Most notably a Mrs. Beaupre, whose name I pronounced "Booper" after a long pause and some stammering, which caused Carter, who was sitting next to me, to burst out laughing, which caused me to then join him and hang up the phone in a panic.)

So I'm afraid we were not very productive. Rather, we found our fun in trying to find new ways to crack each other up, or sabotage Matt's political future in his absence, or shock and embarrass any of the earnest young Democrats unfortunate enough to be trapped inside a building with us.

One of the walls in the phone bank room had been covered in paper and turned into a bulletin board where staffers and volunteers hung banners and pinned pictures and wrote messages to rally the troops: "Keep up the fight!" "Latest poll: Kerrey gaining among undecideds!" Stuff like that. I decided to get in on the rah-rah spirit and add a few words of my own.

That was poor judgment on my part. What I wrote was very silly. I believe I used the phrase *compromising positions*. And it was not true. Not to the best of my knowledge anyway. You were the front-runner at the time (or was it Paul Tsongas?). Whatever the case, you were leading Kerrey. And aspects of your personal life had recently come into play. The

Gennifer Flowers story was the talk of the town. I didn't know what was true or not. I didn't care. I just thought the folks at Kerrey HQ might enjoy a little topical humor at the competition's expense.

They didn't, if it makes you feel any better. Awhile after I returned to my seat next to Carter, someone in charge came in, having been alerted to the presence of my note, and angrily asked who'd done it. It must have been fairly obvious from our giggling. "There's press around," she said, crossing out the words in heavy black marker. "Don't be stupid."

Turned out, of course, that you were a really good president. And seeing as how you wound up in such hot water for certain transgressions that hewed uncomfortably close to those I fabricated that day in 1992 and how Kenneth Starr put your personal business out there in that report for everyone in the world to read—well, I don't much like the thought of being in league with Kenneth Starr. That guy's a jerk.

■ ■ ■

Dear T.,

Sorry for telling you what I was thinking about when you asked me what I was thinking about.

There are times in life when we should lie. This—junior year of college, lying in your bed, having just had sex with you—was one of those times.

Your dorm room was so clean and neat with pink stuff and flower prints. It smelled nice, too. Like soft spices. What had I done to deserve even being there? I'd picked my clothes out of a bathtub-size pile on my floor. You were pretty and dressed nicely and seemed to have yourself much more together. By dint of beer and dumb luck, you'd started kissing me at a party a few weeks earlier. A friend of yours lived next to a friend of mine. We'd all gone out as a group, got very drunk, got to dancing. You stumbled back to my room with me and we fell into bed. I was painfully hungover the next day, and I had to go to New Hampshire to volunteer for Bob Kerrey's primary campaign, which turned out to be a mistake. I smiled the whole drive up, though, while my friends teased me. Women didn't fall into my bed as often as I would have liked them to.

There were reasons for this other than my wearing dirty clothes. I had chosen to major in philosophy (shorter reading assignments, higher tolerance for half-informed guesswork in class discussions) and became deeply invested in telling the truth. Too invested. I had read this book, *I and Thou* by Martin Buber, that talked about the great importance of open and honest and thoughtful communication, that this is the only way to show respect for other people as our equals. At least, that's what I thought it was about. It's likely that I misunderstood a lot of what Buber actually meant. But I got off on it. I started seeing telling the truth as the most important thing in the world. Truth, as I conceived it existing in some a priori ideal form, was the ultimate good, the closest thing to god, I suppose, that I believed in. Honesty was the noblest thing a human could aspire to, a spiritual duty. I thought that any lie, no matter how small or how justified by earthly circumstances, was essentially wrong. I remember arguing to my friend Becca that had I lived in the apartment downstairs from Anne Frank in Amsterdam in 1942, though I thought that I would have probably lied to Nazi soldiers if they came asking questions, I also thought that, in the grand scheme of things, my doing so would have hurt the universe in some perhaps indiscernible but important way. It's so embarrassing to think about now. Like the sound of my lying voice was going to bore a hole in the sky and burn a "minus one" mark on the collective soul—which I envisioned as a glowing blue orb of pure, undiluted Truth. *Oy vey.*

So while I didn't feel compelled to voice my every true feeling—I didn't go around telling strangers I thought their shirts were ugly—I tried hard to never lie. Not even a little bit. Needless to say, it was impractical. And exhausting. One time a new friend, Jim, had come to my dorm room to hang out. I mentioned that another friend, Todd, was supposed to be calling—we had plans. "Oh, don't tell him I'm here," Jim said. I forget why. Nothing important. But before I could explain to Jim how difficult this seemingly easy request would be for me, the phone rang. "Hey, Todd," I said as Jim held his finger to his lips. Todd asked me what I was doing. "Nothing. Hanging out." I paused, struggling, and said, "Jim's here." Jim's jaw dropped and I mouthed him an "I'm sorry." After I hung up, he asked me why I had done that. When I explained, he thought I was pulling his leg. "Come on," he said. "You *never* lie?" Then he cracked up, like I had just told a good joke. It does seem pretty funny, looking back.

But what a terribly selfish way to behave. What business was it of mine if Jim didn't want Todd to know where he was? Like I couldn't have endured such a triviality in order to spare him what must have been a bit of discomfort, no matter how minor, the next time they spoke. I was living by a code that amounted to imposing my beliefs on other people. Like a religious zealot. Yuck.

And you got the worst of it. We were having fun, sleeping together every other night or so. The kind of good, healthy, casual fun lots of coeds enjoy often and often with the same partner for more than a couple weeks at a time. But here's a truth that I'm more aware of now than I was then: I was still in love with my old girlfriend from high school, who had dumped me and broken my heart more than a year before. One would think having new sex with different people might have served as a curative in this regard. But these things are rarely simple. Despite how stoned and ragamuffin I imagine I looked to others, I couldn't really do anything casually at that point in my life. Not even have fun. I was wound too tight, strung too high. And because of the vision quest I took myself to be on at this middle-range liberal arts school in Connecticut, I brought my hang-ups into your bed.

We were lying there, sweaty and quiet, our heads on your pillows, when you said, "What are you thinking about?"

Now, as notorious as this question is—I believe it was another philosopher, Andrew Dice Clay, who once said, "If I wanted you to know, I'd be talking…"—it really shouldn't be that big a deal. And it's understandable that it would be asked. It's quiet. Two people getting to know each other in an intimate situation, the silence starts to take on a weight; you want to make conversation. It shouldn't have been that big a deal, even if I didn't want to tell you what I was thinking. I could have said, "Nothing," for example. That would have been fine. Or I could have just made something up, switched my focus to another thought: "It smells nice in here." "Who painted that picture of the flowers?" "I'm supposed to read such and such for class tomorrow." Whatever.

It was really not okay for me to leave the question hanging for as long as I did and then say, "I was thinking I was worried about your feelings being hurt. Because I don't know that I see this relationship lasting very long."

I thought I was being good and noble and respecting you more as a person by telling the whole, honest, undiluted truth. I was not. I was being an asshole.

■ ■ ■

Dear Julia Neaman,

I'm sorry for accusing you of conspiring against me when I was on hallucinogenic mushrooms.

This was in May 1992, the last week of spring semester,

when the seniors at our college were preparing to graduate. Senior Week, they called it, every night of which there was a different party thrown by juniors to celebrate the achievement. You were in charge of one of those parties, the school having given you a budget based on a proposal you'd submitted. You'd chosen me to be on your twenty-person party staff—something of an honor in that it allowed an underclassman to attend an otherwise seniors-only party, and also just nice of you because we didn't know each other very well. We'd just met that year in Mr. Vogel's modern philosophy course.

The responsibilities of party staff were vague. Cart sound-system equipment? Serve seniors beer? Stand guard at an inflatable trampoline? Nothing too taxing, you assured.

It was beautiful weather the day of the party, so I spent the afternoon lying on my back in the garden behind the Asian studies building, tripping on mushrooms with a bunch of my friends, letting my sense of time and selfhood dissipate like the puffy white clouds floating in the sky above. It was totally awesome.

When the sun got low, someone mentioned dinner. Food seemed like an entirely foreign concept to me at the time, but we all got up off the grass and headed back to central campus. When we got to the quad, where the party was to be held, I saw you standing in the middle of a group of people, setting things up. Realizing that I was supposed to be there working, I said good-bye to my friends and walked over.

You were busy. You said hello but had to see to a more

pressing matter, so I just stood there by the tent that had been erected between the old stone dorm buildings, watching its shadow slant across the huge slabs of granite and thinking about how they'd been mortared into place so long before I was born. I didn't know many of the other people working the party but eventually found myself standing with Brad, who'd also been in our philosophy class, and a guy named Shane, who was on the sailing team. There didn't seem to be anything for us to do setup wise, so Brad and Shane asked if I'd like to go to Shane's room and smoke pot. This seemed like a good idea but was not.

Soon after we smoked, the tapestry-draped, cinder-block dorm room began to feel extremely cramped. There was nowhere to sit. Brad and Shane were talking about stuff I couldn't understand. I wondered at some point whether they'd made up a secret language. But I nodded along so as to be polite.

We left around eight o'clock or so. It was a great relief to get outside. But by that time, it was beginning to get dark and the road back to the quad had taken on a sinister air. I still had no idea what Brad and Shane were saying when they spoke. And when they laughed, it was worse.

Back at the tent, the party had started. Seniors were arriving, drunk and loud as they'd been all week. You were a whirl of orchestrating activity, talking fast, with people surrounding you wherever you went. I didn't dare approach. Brad and Shane, though, went to get their assignments and were soon stationed at the side of the stage, ten feet behind an orange rope. There would be a band playing later, and I guess they were supposed to keep people away from the instruments or something. It was all very confusing. I walked around by myself for a while, and it soon became clear that everyone was against me.

So I probably had a scowl on my face when you found me, standing someplace apart from the crowd. If so, you didn't mind and smiled friendly when you asked if I had a desk lamp in my room.

"A *desk lamp*?" I said, as if I couldn't conceive of such a thing. I couldn't actually. It took me a minute to visualize what a desk lamp, in fact, was.

"Yeah," you said. "Is there one in your room?"

"A desk lamp."

"Yeah." You giggled. "A lamp on your desk."

I did have one. Right on my desk. Like most college students do.

"Yeah," I said cautiously. "I have a desk lamp." I was suspicious. What could you possibly need a desk lamp for?

"Could you get it?"

"Yeah," I said. "I guess so."

"Thanks!" You were cheery. As you usually were. You're a very nice person. But I was not in a cheery mood. And I could only imagine ulterior motives.

You stepped away, leaving me bewildered. Why would you ask me for a desk lamp? I couldn't think of a reason.

But I started back to my dorm. I was supposed to be working for you. You ask me for a desk lamp, I'll get one.

Walking across campus, I racked my brain. What could it be? Gradually it came to me: you were setting me up for public humiliation. I was to walk all the way to my room, unplug my desk lamp, and carry it all the way back to the party, at which time you would point at me, standing there with an unwieldy desk lamp in my hand, and shout, "Ha-ha! Look, everybody! Dave has a lamp in his hand!" And then, since there would certainly be no place to put a desk lamp at a party, I'd have to lug it around with me for the rest of the night—marked as a dupe. I even imagined that I'd heard of this before. That it was a hazing ritual at certain college fraternities. (Our college had no fraternities.) That pledges were made to carry their desk lamps with them wherever they went for the duration of Hell Week and that they'd be punished severely if found without one. (I do think a similar tradition may in fact take place in fraternities. But probably not with desk lamps.)

By the time I'd gotten to my dorm, I'd convinced myself that I was the butt of a well-known party gag. Everyone knew I had taken too many drugs, everyone was waiting for me to get back there, and they were all going to have a big laugh when they saw me with the lamp in my hand. You would be high-fiving with someone. I was resigned to it.

I walked into my friend Will's room. Will was a senior and was getting ready to go to the party. He was showered and relaxed in clean clothes. He could tell something was wrong as soon as he saw me.

"Why so glum, chum?" he asked.

"I fell for the old lamp trick," I said sadly.

"The what?"

"You know, the thing where someone asks you to bring a lamp to a party. And then there's no place to put the lamp, so you end up holding the lamp in your hands all night."

Will gently assured me I was out of my mind. I went upstairs and got the lamp, and we walked back to the party together. The band had started playing, people were dancing. I found you and presented the lamp. To my surprise, you took it. But when you walked away, I assumed I'd just lost a lamp. "Yeah, like she needs a *lamp* at a *party*," I said to Will.

Ten minutes later, Will pulled my shirt. "Come here," he said. "There's something you should see."

He walked me over to a folding table set up near the back of the tent. My lamp was sitting on it, shining its light on an array of cassette tapes of the band that was playing. A ska band from Boston. Chucklehead, they were called. The tapes were for sale. "See?" said Will.

I think everyone but me had a really good time at the party.

■ ■ ■

Dear Aunt Ava,

I'm sorry for breaking Pa's sculpture.

It was made of a solid, dark wood. Around two feet tall, an oval-shaped figure rising off a square block base, vaguely representational of a mother cradling her child, it was one of my favorite sculptures of his. He'd had it on the mantel of the fireplace in his living room, under one of the golden angels mounted on the chimney. He was a good sculptor, Pa.

I had driven to your parents' house in West Orange to pick it up on my way to my friend Jim's house in nearby Montclair, where I was set to spend the night. Pa had told me that I could choose a sculpture of his to display in my dorm room that fall, so after a short visit, a cup of coffee, and a zwieback, I carried it out to the car and laid it on my duffel bag on the passenger seat—I wanted to give it a cushion.

Having something that Pa had made was important to me. Your brother, my father, had died a year and a half before, and we'd all been knocked off balance. My mother, always clear-eyed and stoic, kept herself busy with work and taking care of Debby and the house, but fell into social isolation. Debby was doing great in lots of ways. She attended an adolescent bereavement group, I know, and got very into modern dance and did well in school and had a strong group of friends. But at her bat mitzvah, when you got up and asked the congregation for a moment of silence in honor of my dad—which was a nice thing to do, of course—I looked over at her, standing so poised in her shiny blue dress, and thought about how unfair it was. I remembered myself at her age, free to invest more emotional energy than was warranted into normal thirteen-year-old concerns like who was the better drummer, Keith Moon or John Bonham (Moon), or how I could get my hair to look the way I wanted it to look (I couldn't), or whether or not to invite Wendy Metzger or any other girls to my bar mitzvah (I didn't. I was such a dork). Debby didn't have that luxury. Even when she smiled, you could see it: she knew a lot more about the heavier stuff than kids her age were supposed to.

Dad's death aged your parents like the passage of time never had before. Your mother, Thea, my grandmother, talked about it in evolutionary psychological terms. "We are designed to bury our parents," she said. "It's a normal part of human existence, the natural order. I buried my mother. That was right. We are not designed to bury our children. When your father died—a mother is not designed to cope with that. It broke something in me."

David Landy came to our house about a week after Dad died. I was glad to see him; I had a question for him. I had gone through Dad's old clothes and taken a bunch of stuff that I thought I might wear—belts, T-shirts, sweaters, his suede coat from the '60s. But I'd felt weird doing it. The phrase *grave robber* occurred to me. I asked my mother what she thought, and she recommended I talk to David Landy. His father had died a couple years before. So right away, right as I answered the door, I explained the situation and asked him, "What do you think my dad would have thought?"

He put his hand on my shoulder. "I wear something that belonged to my father every day," he said. "I think that it would make your dad happy to think about you wearing his clothes. In fact, I know it. It would make him proud. I cherish the things I have from my father. For me, wearing something of my father's is like a way of keeping him with me a little bit."

Pa's statue served a similar talismanic function for me. He was getting very old, in his eighties. I'm not sure whether or not he'd had his first heart attack yet, but it was around that time. I was reading Marx and Max Weber and Freud in college and coming to appreciate our family's history—Pa's role in the Socialist resistance movement against Hitler's rise, Thea's work as a first wave psychoanalyst—in ways that I had not before. Laying on the duffel bag next to me as I started the car and pulled out of the driveway on Shady Glen, the sculpture's elegant curves, the dark stain that brought out the patterns in the wood's grain, the patience and care so evident in the carving, all this spoke to something in Pa that I liked to think was in me, in my blood. It was beautiful. I was proud.

But I was not a good driver. I have never been good with directions. At that time of my life, my mental state was like the water in a snow globe just after you shake it up, the bits of glitter swirling in all directions before settling into their downward drift. I was always feeling frantic, even when I might have looked calm from the outside.

So navigating myself to an unfamiliar address always threw me into a panic. This was the case with Jim's house. I had written directions; it should have been a ten-minute drive. But after pulling off Harrison Avenue, I found myself lost in the maze of same-looking streets that make up northern New Jerseyan suburbia. I was on a commercial strip, passing the small, manicured lawns and parking lots out in front of banks, Italian delis, Laundromats, etc., shouting curses at my feeble brain as I peered out the passenger side window and struggled to read the street signs, when I glanced back in front of me and saw that I was coming up on a line of cars stopped at a red light. Coming up much too fast.

I jammed on the brakes and heard the tires squeal, felt my seat belt pull tight across my chest. The sculpture flew off the duffel bag and smashed into the dashboard with a crack. I was lucky it didn't hit the windshield. I was lucky I didn't hit the car in front of me.

"Fucking idiot!" I shouted. The sculpture lay on the floor in front of the passenger seat.

When I finally found Jim's house and pulled into his driveway and parked, I unbuckled my seat belt and reached down and picked up the sculpture and turned it over in my hands. I wasn't expecting it to be broken. It was a thick, solid block of wood. But there it was: the lovely, smooth curve Pa had cut and sanded and polished with his hands—split down the middle like a tree after a lightning storm. I ran my finger along the crack, felt the sharp splinters.

I slammed the heel of my palm against the steering wheel hard enough to hurt. I yanked at my hair with my hands. I felt like I might cry. I didn't. But I sat there for a long time before going inside.

The next day when I drove home, I put the duffel bag and the sculpture back on the passenger seat. This time, I thought to use the seat belt to strap it down. But it was already broken.

Pa died four years later, in 1996. You have a lot of his artwork in your house in Boston. You've taken up sculpting in the past few years yourself. You work with clay, and some of your pieces remind me of his. I don't know where the sculpture of the mother and child is. Maybe in the basement of my mom's house; I never wanted to throw it away. I should bring it up to you next Thanksgiving. Maybe you could fill in the crack with clay. It wouldn't be the same as the original. But it could be nice.

■ ■ ■

Dear Nick,

I'm sorry I ate your carrot cake.

We were at college and living off campus in the house on Bragaw Street. You had bought the cake earlier that day, when we'd all gone to Super Stop & Shop for groceries. It was a small piece, an individual serving, wrapped in cellophane. You'd paid for it separately and left it in the fridge while you went to an afternoon class. But our roommate Scott and I didn't have afternoon classes that day. Or if we did, we decided to skip them and stay home and smoke pot instead. Whatever the case, we stayed home while you were out and smoked pot. I got hungry, on account of the pot smoking, and went to the fridge, where I found the carrot cake. I knew it was yours. I knew you were saving it to eat later. I don't even like carrot cake that much. Still, it looked good with that thick layer of cream cheese frosting on top, and self-discipline has never been a strong suit of mine. I decided to have just one little bite. Then I ate the whole thing.

You came home and looked in the fridge and came into the living room where Scott and I and Pete from downstairs were sitting and asked what had happened to the carrot cake. I told you I had eaten it. You were angry—as well you should have been. That was very inconsiderate of me.

But that's not the worst of it. As you've pointed out many times since that day (as somehow, miraculously, we've remained friends), what really made you as mad as you ended up being was the fact that I refused to admit any wrongdoing.

"You know this is a house where people smoke pot," I said. "You know people tend to get hungry when they smoke pot. It's unreasonable to expect a piece of carrot cake left alone in a fridge near where pot is being smoked won't be eaten. Under the standard conditions of this house, I can't take responsibility for what happens to a piece of carrot cake." I smiled a stoned smile at you while you frowned—so obviously not stoned. "Especially," I continued, just to be a dick, "a piece of carrot cake as delicious as that one was." You called me a dick and turned around and went back into the kitchen. Scott and Pete were laughing. I sat there, happy with myself for constructing such an ironclad argument. I felt like a lawyer. Like Sam Waterston.

Embarrassingly, thinking back, a good part of me actually believed that what I said had some merit. Like since we smoked so much pot, we somehow lived under a different code: the Pot Rules, unbeholden to logic or common decency. I'll slough responsibility again now and blame the environment: our life at that college was just that divorced from reality. Tuition paid for by our parents, the extent of our responsibilities being to show up for, what, eight hours of classes a week? Make it to a professor's office at some point and ask for another extension on an overdue philosophy paper? How could we not fall into spoiled, utopian thinking? But god, in hindsight, what an ugly utopia. Where any self-indulgent doofus is free to rationalize away transgression so long as there's a couple other doofuses there to laugh along with him. (I believe there may have been a *Star Trek* episode along these lines...) Where right and wrong can be spun out of thin air and "pack the bong" is the last word on any subject.

So I officially apologize. I hereby accept full responsibility for my actions. And I owe you a piece of carrot cake.

NEW YORK

(Or Stumbling into the Real World.)

Dear Afrika Baby Bam,

I'm sorry I used the word *fiending* in conversation with you.

I must have sounded like such a dork. It's not a word I usually use.

This was summer 1994. I was an intern at *Vibe* magazine, which was a new magazine then, not yet a year old. I had come down to New York City from college in Connecticut to stay at my friend Will's apartment for two months—his roommate Joey was away for the summer. Every morning I would report to the offices on Lexington Avenue, where I would sort mail and transcribe interview tapes and read through the local newspapers looking for hip-hop-related stories, which I would cut out and photocopy and staple into ten or twelve easily digestible packets to be distributed to the editors and editorial assistants. I was happy to be there. I loved hip-hop; I loved all types of music. I'd wanted to be a music writer since I was in high school. (I'd written record reviews for the school paper my senior year: Full of fawning clichés about Keith Richards's *Talk Is Cheap* and Lou Reed's *New York*. Full of sub-clever snark about Europe's *The Final Countdown*.) Even in its infancy, I thought *Vibe* was about the best music magazine going. And I found that I really liked the people who worked there.

You were, as you know, a hip-hop star. A founding member of the rap group the Jungle Brothers, as well as the beloved and important collective of boho artists known as the Native Tongues. You and your partners Mike G and Sammy B, De La Soul, A Tribe Called Quest, I had been listening to you guys, loving your music, for years.

So I was very excited the day that *Vibe*'s music editor, Danyel Smith, the editor at the magazine that I had become closest with, gave me the special assignment of calling you to get a comment for a story she was working on. I forget what it was about. Queen Latifah maybe—another Native Tongues cohort.

You hadn't put out any new music in a while. Your first two albums, *Straight out the Jungle* and *Done by the Forces of Nature*, had come out in the '80s and were—and are—stone classics. (I'm listening to the latter as I type this, and it sounds as terrific as ever.) Your third album, *J Beez wit the Remedy*, was marked by conflict you were having with your record company, Warner Bros. As the story went, you guys wanted to go in a more experimental direction, and the executives balked. The final product suffered for the discord, and the album didn't sell. Your fans (like me!) were hoping for a comeback.

Danyel said I should ask about this after getting a suitable quote for the Latifah story (or whatever the topic was). "And ask him what's up with the JBs," she said. "What are they working on? When might we hear some new music? Maybe we can get a Start piece out of it." (Start was the name of the front section of the magazine—full of smaller, newsy items.)

I took a pen and notepad into the fact-checker's room, a square, windowless space in the center of the offices where there was an empty cubicle and a phone I could use. I had never interviewed anyone for the magazine before. Dialing the number Danyel had given me, I was nervous.

But you were totally cool and down-to-earth. We talked about Latifah or whatever it was for a couple minutes, and you gave me a quote Danyel could plug into the story. And then we started to talk about the Jungle Brothers. I expressed my admiration, and you were gracious, and I gingerly mentioned the record company drama and you talked about that for a while, and then I tried to ask you about the possibility of new music.

"So what about some new Jungle Brothers music?" I started. "Everybody's..."

And then my mind went blank. I couldn't think of a word to express the idea that your fans were eager to hear a new album. I should have said just that: "eager." Or "hoping" or "anticipating" or even simply "we can't wait." There are lots of things I could have said that would have worked just fine. But none of them occurred to me.

The only word that came to mind was a hip-hop slang term. One that I had only recently become aware of. I'd heard it in the lyrics to rap songs and around the *Vibe* offices, too. But it was relatively new to the lexicon. It was the word *fiend-*

ing. Usually pronounced with a clipped final *g*, so *fiendin'*, it came from the term "dope fiend," or more modernly, "crack fiend," and referred to a feeling of strong desire—a desire that matched a drug addict's need for his or her next hit of drugs. A need so strong as to lead a person to commit evil deeds. Hyperbolic, sure. But I liked it. *Fiend* is such a great-sounding word.

I had never before used it in conversation, though. I had been a rap music fan for a long time—since the mid-1980s when Run-DMC broke—but I'd never adopted much hip-hop slang into daily use. Even the most common, mainstream examples, *fresh*, or *diss*, or *yo*, generally felt funny coming out of my mouth. I had grown up in the suburbs and attended a small New England liberal arts college and didn't like the thought of pretending to be someone that I was not.

But I was stuck midsentence, floundering, and the pause was getting too long. So I did the best I could. "Everybody's...really, umm...*fiending* for a new Jungle Brothers album."

I cringed when I said it. I sounded like Officer Hopkins from *Sanford and Son*, the super-square cop who always made clumsy attempts at hip jive talk. ("Right up!" instead of "right on," etc.) I was glad you could not see me and glad that I was not using a tape recorder.

You weren't fazed. You didn't laugh at me or anything. You said you guys were working on new music but didn't know when it would come out. I thanked you for your time and we hung up.

I rewrote the quote that I had jotted down for Danyel's story on a fresh page of the notebook, ripped it out, and carried it to her office.

"How did it go?" she asked from her desk.

"Fine, I think," I said, handing her the piece of paper. "Except..." I started to laugh at myself and shook my head. "I told him everybody was really *fiending* for the new music."

"You're stupid, Bry."

She said it in an affectionate way. But she was right, too.

■ ■ ■

Dear Residents of 208 East Seventh Street,

Sorry for leaving that couch outside our door on the fourth-floor stairwell for two weeks.

We were just moving into the building, my friend Tim and I, fall of 1995. I had graduated college that spring and this was the first apartment I'd ever officially leased. And I didn't know a lot about neighborly etiquette. Or making a good first impression.

The couch did not completely block the stairwell or access to the short hallway off which our door opened. It was off to the side, tipped up on an armrest, leaning vertically against the wall. Obviously, we would have preferred it to be inside our apartment. It was a long, cushioned couch upholstered with stripes of velour in various shades

of green. Tim had bought it for twenty dollars at a sec-
ondhand furniture place near where he'd grown up outside
of Syracuse and driven it down the weekend we moved
in. We had carried it up three flights of steps and then
struggled for at least an hour, sweating and cursing pro-
fusely, trying every possible angle and alignment to get it
through our door, which opened awkwardly, infuriatingly,
into a much-too-thin interior hallway. We unscrewed the
legs of the couch, we took the door off its hinges, hoping
than any extra inch of leeway would make the difference.
It didn't. We had nowhere to store the couch while we figured out what to do next. We were exhausted. So we left it
there.

We discussed the possibility of bringing it back down to
the street and leaving it for someone else to take. But we
really liked the couch. And Tim had come so far with it. It
was hard to accept defeat.

Days passed. Then a week. We were not very good problem solvers, Tim and I.

We were aware that the situation was suboptimal. Two
white kids, fresh out of college, moving into a heavily black
and Latino neighborhood; it was early in the Clinton boom
years, and there was a lot of talk about gentrification in the
East Village at the time; we knew that we were part of an
unpopular wave. The last thing we would have wanted to do
was annoy anyone.

But sure enough, one day during the second week the
couch was out there, I came home to find a piece of paper

taped to it with words written in black Magic Marker. "Move this couch," it said. "Slave days are over."

Completely reasonable. (Though it feels important to say that we were not expecting anybody else to handle this problem for us.) Also, a thank-you, to whichever one of our neighbors wrote the sign, for using the piece of paper.

I took the sign inside and replaced it with a similar one saying, "Sorry—will move soon," and Tim and I gave ourselves one more day, two tops, to try to figure out a way to get the couch inside. Might we be able to bring the couch up onto the roof and lower it down with rope and pull it in through a window? We measured the windows. Nope.

I had given up and was advocating that Tim do the same, when his friend Armin came up with an idea. Armin lived nearby. He was a photo researcher for *The New Yorker* and competent in a way that Tim and I were clearly not.

The next night, he showed up at our door with a toolbox. We flipped the couch over so that its legs were facing up. Armin took out an X-Acto knife and slit the underside cloth down the middle. We held the flaps open while he inspected the structure—there were lots of springs inside and metal bars and wood. Then he took a small saw out of his box and sawed one piece of wood in half. One piece of wood, out of the whole inscrutable mess of furniture guts, and *voilà*! Our heavy, sturdy, previously rigid ten-foot couch bent like an accordion. How had he done it? Had he studied couch design? Had he gone to carpentry school? "No." Armin shrugged. "I don't know. It's no big deal."

Funny how different people's brains work so differently. I would not have thought to do that in a million years. And even if I had thought of it, the execution would have been way beyond me. I am not technically inclined.

Needless to say, a flexible couch is much more easily moved around corners. We brought it in through our door, down the hall past the bathroom, carried it in through the kitchen, and into our living room—where Armin then braced the piece of wood he'd sawed with two smaller pieces of wood (a ruler, I think, and a paint stirrer) and duct taped it back together, good as new. The front of the couch had a little curtain that hung to the floor, so we didn't even have to sew up the cut cloth.

Tim and Armin fell out of touch shortly after that. But Armin has remained, for me, one of those people you pass on the sidewalk or spot in a crowded bar more frequently than you do other people—the kismet of similar routes and schedules. For seventeen years now, I've been seeing him what seems like at least once or twice a year, even as I've moved to different neighborhoods and changed jobs and stuff. We've long since stopped saying hello to each other; he'd likely not even recognize me. I saw him just last week actually at a Mets game. I was there with my kid; he was standing on line for hot dogs with two kids of his own. (Or maybe his kid and a friend of his kid's?) I didn't wave and he didn't notice me. But as I do every time I see him, I thought to myself, *That guy's smart!*

It's interesting how, in the city, people so easily drift in and out of other people's lives. When anonymity is generally assumed and expected, people can go from being strangers to friends to strangers again without any hassles or hang-ups or hurt feelings. It's a good thing. Of course, as I write this, I wonder if any of you see me from time to time without my knowing it. Maybe I've stopped recognizing you as Armin has done with me. What do you think to yourself when you see me? I bet it's something other than *That guy's smart.*

■ ■ ■

Dear LexisNexis On-site Training Executive,

I'm sorry you had to learn my secret password.

You were just doing your job, back in 1996, visiting the offices of companies that had recently purchased accounts with the new computer database of newspaper articles and legal papers called LexisNexis. I was working as a freelance fact-checker in the research department at *Vibe* magazine. LexisNexis was an invaluable research tool. *Vibe* ponied up.

A week or so after we fact-checkers had been granted access to the service, you arrived at our office to give us a day's worth of tutoring in how to most efficiently use it. You were pert and pretty, ten years older than most of us, your square-shouldered navy suit out of place among our sagging jeans and T-shirts. But you were not shy, and after a short lecture and demonstration, you walked around our windowless work space, coming to each of our computers, watching over our shoulders, offering helpful bits of advice.

I was having trouble. Unable to find an article, I'd gotten myself stuck somewhere in the database web and couldn't find my way back to the start of my search session.

You came over to talk me through the problem but were soon frowning, flummoxed as I was. It didn't surprise me that I'd found a new and challenging way to get lost in a computer system; I've never been good with machines. "Here," you said, motioning to the keyboard. "Let me sit down." I got up and stood behind you while you started pressing buttons.

"You know what," you said. "Let's just start over." You typed a combination of keys and the screen blinked back to the log-in page. *That's better*, I thought.

Then, still looking at the screen, you asked, "What's your password?"

I felt myself turn red. All the pores on my skin opened at once. "Ummm," I said, stalling. "My password?"

"Yeah." You turned to me. "So we can log back in."

"Ummm, it's…" I couldn't think fast enough. I should have said I'd forgotten it. I should have made up something new and blamed a typo or a computer glitch and just shrugged when it wouldn't work.

You looked at me blankly.

I started to sweat. "It's…ummm…It's silly," I said with a desperate giggle. "I guess I should have…It's bad."

You raised your eyebrows.

I didn't know what to do. "It's...ummm..." I couldn't think of any way out of it. Other people were starting to look. Stiffening my lip, I lowered my voice and told you.

"Horsedick."

I'd like to say that this was an old nickname of mine. It was not. It was a reference to a favorite joke, a cartoon I'd seen in a *Playboy* magazine someone had snuck into school back in fifth grade or so. A middle-aged man opens the door to his suburban house to find a hulking young brute standing there with flowers in his hand. "Tell Sally Horsedick's here," says the caption. (I'd always assumed Sally to be the man's daughter. But thinking about it now, I suppose she could have been meant to be his wife. Either way—kinda funny, right? Okay.)

I hadn't had a lot of experience with computer passwords up to that point in my life. It had never occurred to me that I might one day find myself in a situation where I'd have to share mine with an attractive older woman in a business suit. It was supposed to be secret, after all.

To your eternal credit, you were very cool. Nothing if not professional.

You shook your head, turned back to the screen, set your hands on the keyboard, and sighed. "One word or two?"

■ ■ ■

Dear Everlast from House of Pain,

I'm sorry for calling you a "Leprechaun of Rage."

This was in a review I wrote for *Vibe* magazine of the third and last House of Pain album, *Truth Crushed to Earth Shall Rise Again*.

It was not a very nice thing to say, especially there where I put it, in the first line of the piece. "Make way for the Leprechauns of Rage," I said. It was a reference to the Public Enemy song "Prophets of Rage," of course. You guys being an Irish American rap group rather than black, like Public Enemy and most other rap groups. It seems less clever to me now than it did at the time. But I guess that's the thing about getting older, huh?

I said lots of other not-so-nice things in the review, too. It wasn't a very good album. By way of comparison, it didn't "bang like shillelaghs," as I said the first two House of Pain albums did. (I'm not sure that that could have ever sounded clever. But I did mean it; I really like those albums.) I criticized your lyrics and the beats you used and insinuated that the group's prior success might have been reliant on your former executive producer, Cypress Hill's DJ Muggs. I threw a couple more Irish jokes in at the end, too.

It was early in my career. I'd just started writing record reviews. People liked the pans, I'd noticed, and snide wit. Also, I'd grown up not Irish in a heavily Irish town, among a heavily Irish circle of friends who liked to crack back and forth about matters of ethnicity. So when I was assigned to review an album from a rap group that had always been very vocal about its Irishness, and when I didn't like that album, I got my knives out. In my mind, I was back in the Red Bank Regional lunchroom with Matt McCabe, Ted O'Brien, Mark McCarthy.

Was there an even uglier impulse? Did the glee I took in attacking your album have to do with the fact that I was a white guy at a largely black magazine writing about a bunch of other white guys in hip-hop? Did I use the opportunity to take you down a peg as a way to earn some kind of stripes? I'd like to think not. Not consciously. But might there've been just a smidgen of that slipping in there with those jokes? I wonder.

You read the review when it came out. I shouldn't have found that surprising, but I did—and strangely flattering, the thought of a rap star, someone I'd seen on MTV, sitting there reading words I had written. But you didn't appreciate my criticisms or, apparently, find my jokes very funny. I know all this because both your publicist at the time and a friend of mine at the magazine who was friends with some of your friends told me you had spoken about wanting to beat me up.

Coincidentally, your album and my review of it came out around the same time as the movie *Swingers* with Vince Vaughn and Jon Favreau. As I'm sure you're aware, there's a scene in that movie where a friend of the protagonists shocks everybody by pulling out a gun during a shouting match with a bunch of white hip-hop heads. Vince Vaughn admonishes him for overreacting. "Like fuckin' House of Pain was gonna do anything?" he says. So I can understand why you might have been extra cranky those days.

According to reports from the friends of my friend, you were the type of guy who most certainly *would* have done something. So I'm grateful that your publicist fended off your requests that he bring you to a *Vibe* party and point me out to you. I would likely have ended up picking my teeth out of a platter of vegetable spring rolls.

When the album flopped and House of Pain broke up sometime in the next year, people around the office joked that my review was like the famous one Jon Landau wrote in *Rolling Stone* that convinced Eric Clapton to disband Cream in 1968. I knew that was unlikely the case in this instance, but the feeling I got from even just the idea pushed past flattering into something that made me uncomfortable. Things got worse soon thereafter, when news broke that you had suffered a coronary attack that almost killed you. You were unconscious in the hospital for three days, I learned, while surgeons replaced a valve in your heart. You were twenty-nine.

Thankfully, you are a resilient person. Not only did you recover quickly from the surgery, you switched directions musically and scored a major hit with a jangly acoustic-rock tune, "What It's Like." Your solo album, *Whitey Ford Sings the Blues*, sold two million copies. A couple years later, you had that song with Santana on that album of his that sold like twenty million copies: "Put Your Lights On." You won a Grammy for that one. I'm sure you have enough money to last you the rest of your life. I'd imagine you don't often think about record reviews from thirteen years ago.

But still, it was stupid what I did. Not to criticize the album, but to do it so mean-spiritedly. It was the mistake of a young writer feeling himself a little too much. Not taking his job seriously enough, not understanding what it means to put something in print. There's a responsibility that comes with publishing directly related to the fact that the words you write are being read by a circle of people wider than your three best friends from high school. It's more important to refrain from taking cheap shots.

So now, seriously, sorry.

■ ■ ■

Dear Jen,

I'm sorry I said your allergies were psychosomatic.

We were visiting San Francisco in 1997, staying with my old college roommates Drew, Pete, and Scott. We'd slept at our friend Becca's place the night before but left because you were allergic to her cat. You hadn't slept well and you were in a sour mood. We both were. It had been a long day, and we'd been arguing all through it. We were often arguing back then. We are still often arguing actually. This has always been the nature of our relationship: we are close, arguing friends. "It's too hot out," I'll say. "Oh, I like this weather," you'll say.

I was spreading a futon mattress on the living room floor when your sneezing started up again. And coughing and sniffling and wheezing. "Ughh," you said, your nose all red. "The dust. I'm allergic to this whole city."

"You know it's all in your mind," I said.

You dropped the pillow you were holding and looked at me like I'd slapped you.

"What?!"

"I think allergies are largely psychosomatic. Like a manifestation of stress or something."

"*No*," you said, straining for patience, as if you were talking to a five-year-old. "There are tiny particles in the air that I am actually allergic to. And when I breathe them in, they trigger a physical reaction."

I said something that included the phrase *mind over matter*.

"Fuck *you*!" you said, trying to keep your voice low. It was late, we were guests. "Here I am suffering and miserable, and you're going to tell me it's my fault?!"

You were right to be angry. I was being a jerk. Though at the time, I didn't see what I'd said for the attack that it was. Not fully anyway. To some extent, I honestly thought I was trying to help. My father was a psychologist who specialized in pain management through hypnosis. He'd taught me some visualization techniques that were pretty effective at getting rid of headaches and stuff. This combined with the part I always remembered from Stephen King's *It* (that highly regarded medical manual) where one of the kids realizes that

210

his asthma is a symptom of anxiety and cures himself by throwing away his inhaler, and also a general and unfortunate mistrust of science I developed through an overzealous critique of Descartes in a modern philosophy course, and also finding more meaning than there actually is in a line from a Van Morrison song called "Enlightenment" about how we create our own reality—all of this informed what I now believe was an excessive adherence to the notion of mind over matter.

But regardless, it's just not very nice to blame someone for their own suffering. Especially while that suffering is going on. I should have offered nothing but my sympathy that night and brought up my stupid ideas about the power of positive thinking or whatever the next day.

I've been reminded of this a lot in recent springs, whenever I've walked past the corner of Clinton and Rivington Streets on the way back from picking my kid up at school, and been seized by a mysterious coughing fit. I have apparently developed an allergic reaction to the trees growing around there. Mulberries or box elders, and likely a preponderance of males of the species. I read an article in the paper about how the city spent all this money a couple years ago cutting down female trees to lessen the number of flowers or berries that were falling onto sidewalks and cars and making a mess for the Department of Sanitation. And so now when the disproportionate numbers of male trees release their spores in spring, there are fewer receptacles ready to suck them out of the air, and they end up floating around in greater density, giving people allergic reactions. I swear I can actually feel the tiny particles of pollen in my nose, going down my throat, catching to the soft tissue there, forcing the involuntary response. It's miserable.

There's an argument you win.

■ ■ ■

Dear Emily,

I'm sorry for wearing sweatpants to our first dinner date and for getting stoned before meeting your parents for the first time.

This was in 1999. We'd been friends for a couple years at that point, having been introduced by our mutual friend, Jen. We had recently started seeing each other romantically—the result of a particularly drunken night at the WXOU Radio Bar on Hudson Street, near where we all lived in the West Village. I'd asked you out for a first proper dinner date to Hangawi, a fancy Korean restaurant on Thirty-Second Street.

It's funny to think about what I was thinking about as I got ready to meet you. It was a Saturday, and I had been wearing a pair of green sweatpants that I used to wear on weekends. They were the kind that George Costanza used to wear on *Seinfeld*, the kind that Jerry once said announced to the world, "I give up. I can't compete in normal society."

It occurred to me that I might change into something more presentable, but I stood in my bedroom and thought for a minute and decided against it. I put on a white polo shirt and my Converse All Stars and walked out the door. It wasn't that I was trying to feign ambivalence, to give the impression that I didn't care enough to put on pants with buttons and belt loops. I had made it very clear, in fact, that I wanted us to be girlfriend and boyfriend. If anything, you were the one who took some convincing. (Glaringly easy, in hindsight, to see why.) My thinking, as best I can explain it, was more along the lines of *take me as I am.* I was a guy who wore green sweatpants on a Saturday. I wanted to make a good impression, but changing pants for that reason felt wrong. Like I'd be faking it, presenting myself as someone I was not. This type of thinking makes very little sense to me now and is derailed by an argument as simple as the fact that I certainly didn't wear those sweatpants exclusively. I had lots of other pants, many of which I often changed into before dinner without much thought at all. But that day, I felt myself in the hands of fate: *these were the pants you put on this morning; these are the pants you shall wear tonight.* I don't know. I used to be really superstitious, too. And that's just a terrible way to live. I was smoking too much pot those days, I suppose.

Which brings me to the second part of this apology. A couple months later, our relationship having miraculously survived my sweatpants, you'd arranged for us to go to dinner with your parents—my first time meeting them. Bored, sitting around my apartment that afternoon, I came to the same kind of question as before: Here was a situation in which on any other day I would be smoking pot. Should the fact that I was soon to be meeting these important people, the parents of the woman I was falling in love with, should I let that change my routine? I knew that I'd be brighter eyed and clearer in conversation if I refrained, and I definitely wanted your parents to like me. But then I thought, *Well, the way things are going, chances are I'll be spending a lot of time around these people in the future.* There would be lots of days like this. I wasn't planning on making any major changes to my personal lifestyle. They might as well get to know me half lidded and cloudy headed. I packed a bowl.

Dinner went fine. Your parents turned out to be groovy '60s types anyway. Toward the end of the evening, after I recognized a reference one of them made to the Steve Martin–Lily Tomlin movie *All of Me* and mentioned that it was a favorite of mine, your dad said, "Anyone who appreciates *All of Me* is all right by me," and my heart felt warm in my chest. I'd lucked out.

Still, thinking back, it seems pretty stupid. There's a reason most people would choose not to get stoned before meeting their girlfriend's parents. Just like there's a reason to change out of sweatpants before going on a date to a fancy restaurant. Making decisions based on principle rather than pragmatism is a prescription for failure. Even more so when the principle is so confused and self-defeating.

Was all this a test for you? I guess in a way it was, odd as that sounds. Not that I'd meant it that way. But I remember the expression on your face when we met at the restaurant for that first dinner date. You looked down at my sweatpants, and then back up to me, and gave a bemused little sigh. "So this is how it's going to be, huh?" You thought for a second more and said, "All right."

Again, I lucked out.

■ ■ ■

Dear Guy in a Brown Corduroy Jacket,

I'm sorry for stealing forty dollars from your checking account at the ATM in the HSBC Bank on Union Square East.

This was more than ten years ago. Late winter, early spring. It happened around nine p.m. I was meeting some friends to play pool at Corner Billiards on Fourth Avenue, stopping to take out cash on my way. You were coming out of the foyer when I was going in. You looked to be in your late twenties, early thirties, around my age. You were wearing a brown corduroy jacket and green army fatigue pants, and you had a beard. You might very well have been on your way to meet some friends to play pool, too.

I stepped up to the ATM nearest to the door, the one you'd just left, and saw that the screen was asking if you wanted to end the session or make another transaction? I turned around. The door had closed. I saw you through the glass, walking away. I was alone there. Of course, I had found ATM screens left like that before. It's a common mistake—someone has their money, they're done, they walk away. I'd always just pressed End Session and started my own new one. I'd always wondered, though, as I did it, whether or not it would be possible in such a situation to take money out of the open account. That night, unluckily for you, my curiosity got the better of me. Without giving it much thought, I pressed Make Another Transaction. The machine asked if I'd like to make a withdrawal or check the account's balances. I chose withdrawal and was very surprised when the choice of dollar amounts appeared on the screen: How much would I like to steal? Forty dollars? Sixty dollars? A hundred? Two hundred? More? A nervous giggle fluttered in my throat. The thought of two thousand dollars flashed in my mind. But no, this was just an experiment. I was still half expecting to be asked for your pin number when I pressed $40.00. Then the cash came out, just like that, just like it does when I get money from my own account. It all happened very fast.

I don't make a habit of stuff like this. Besides a stretch in high school, when my friends and I would stumble into 7-Eleven four times a weekend and see who could make and eat the most frozen burritos at the serve-yourself microwave station while a designated one of us distracted the counter clerk and purchased a single candy bar, I haven't stolen much in my life. When I was in third grade, my friend Ted Trainor's parents took five of us to the Ground Round on a Friday night for Ted's ninth birthday. I was addicted to video games. *Ms. Pac-Man* had just come out, and I'd quickly played out my allotment of the quarters Ted's father had given us to take to the arcade after dinner. Crowding around one of the machines with a bunch of kids I didn't know, overwhelmed by desire, I snatched one of the quarters off the waiting line atop the joystick panel and slipped it into my pocket. As soon as I stepped away, though, my hair got hot and my stomach seized up in guilt. I don't think I even played the quarter. Trying to seem tough, I told my friends what I'd done. But in the car on the way home, when Peter Arbour blurted it out, and Mr. Trainor said, in a voice I'll never forget, "Not too cool, Dave," I burst into tears. I confessed to my parents when I got home and spent the rest of the weekend in bed, under the covers, wishing I could die.

It wasn't like that that night when I got to Corner Billiards. But in telling my friends the story of my successful withdrawal of your funds, I started by saying that I didn't feel particularly good about it, that it was done out of curiosity rather than avarice. And sure enough, my friend Josh echoed Mr. Trainor's reaction. "Dude," he said with a surprised laugh. "That's not cool!"

Not that it occupied more than two minutes of conversation, not that I've been beating myself up about it since. But if it makes you feel any better, later that night, after I made what is perhaps the greatest pool shot of my life—jumping an opponent's ball with the cue on the way to sinking the eight ball and winning the game—with onlookers whooping and applauding, I slapped five with Josh, who was my partner (we were playing doubles) and felt a sharp twinge shoot up to my elbow. I'd sprained my wrist.

I swear it hurt for like six months.

■ ■ ■

Dear Residents of Hudson Street between Morton and Barrow Streets,

I'm sorry for shouting out my window at that old lady who used to tie her dog up outside Famiglia's pizza shop. And for my embarrassing lack of creativity.

It was early 2001, shortly before we would all have far more to be worrying about than the nuisance of noise pollution. But back in those comparatively carefree days, I was very much bothered by the loud, raspy barking of a dog that was routinely left leashed to a lamppost on Hudson Street, three stories below my bedroom window. It would happen every day at various times: long, long sessions of barking, forty-five minutes, an hour sometimes. After a while, when I'd hear it start up, I would look out my window and see the dog, a medium-sized mutt with dingy, matted fur, looking plaintively in the direction of the deli mart across the alley from Famiglia's pizza shop and barking and barking and barking.

It drove me crazy. I'd been working from home for a couple

years at that point. I was used to the sounds of the city, able to tune most of them out. But something about this particular dog's bark—how sad it sounded, along with its incessancy—got to me in a different way. There was a cruel and inconsiderate dog owner out there, making the lives of at least two living beings worse. I complained a lot about the situation to my girlfriend with whom I shared the apartment and who I would soon marry. But she worked in an office and so heard the barking only on weekends or the rare nighttime episode. And she is generally less bothered by things than I am anyway. Other than her, I didn't know who to appeal to. I'd never actually seen anyone out there tying up the dog.

One day I wrote a note on a piece of yellow legal-pad paper and taped it to the lamppost while the dog was there barking. "Please don't leave this dog tied up here," it said. "It is obviously unhappy and it barks and barks. This is unfair to the neighborhood and unfair to the dog." I felt pretty stupid, seeing it there in my handwriting. I looked down at the dog, who wasn't paying attention to me, and then just walked away.

Nothing changed. Weeks passed.

I was at the end of my rope the night I finally saw her. It was a weeknight and later than usual, ten o'clock or so. Quiet out on Hudson Street, other than the dog's barking, which had been going on for a half an hour. Quiet inside our apartment, too, other than my ranting about the social contract, etc., which had been going on for about as long. Emily was sitting in bed, trying to read. I'd staked out a position at the window, watching the dog, waiting for the owner. When she appeared, sort of waddling out of the deli mart, a short, heavyset woman with gray hair, and stepped to the lamppost and began untying the leash, I jumped up and ran into the bathroom, where the window in the shower provided a more direct angle from which to shout.

I stepped into the tub, the crinkly plastic shower curtain cold and dry as I pushed it aside, and opened the window and stuck out my head. "Hey, lady!" I said and heard Emily questioning my actions from the bedroom. "Don't tie your dog up there anymore! It barks too loud!"

My voice echoed off the buildings, louder than the dog's barking. The old lady didn't even really look up to see where I was. She dismissed me with a sort of "feh"-style wave of her hand and said, in a voice made of cigarettes, "Don't tell me how to care for my animals."

It was like she'd heard it all before—she had, I suppose—but simply did not care. She was super New York; she had bigger problems to worry about.

"Come on, lady...," I started, but she cut me off.

"Ahh, shut up!"

I was stunned. The gall of this person! But standing in my bathtub at ten o'clock at night, craning my neck out the window, all hot in my ears, I didn't know what to say. I thought for a moment before answering.

"No, *you* shut up!" I shouted back.

I shook my head to myself in the pause that followed. I am not very good at shouting at people.

Then the phone rang. I told Emily I'd get it and pushed back the shower curtain and stepped out of the tub and walked into the kitchen where the phone was.

"Hello?"

"Dave?" It was Nick, my old roommate, who now lived in the building next door. On the sixth floor with his girlfriend Eva.

"Hey, Nick." I said.

"Did I just hear you shouting out your window?"

"Oh, man..."

Nick started laughing. "Did you just tell someone, 'No, *you* shut up?'"

■ ■ ■

Dear Neighbor Who Lived at 67 Morton Street, #3B,

I'm sorry you found me asleep in the hallway outside my apartment.

Asleep is a polite term, of course. I was passed out drunk. This was not as many years ago as I wish it was. I was thirty-one years old. Far too old to be found in such a state by someone whose name I didn't know. We were not fraternity brothers at San Diego State University. We were neighbors. Grown men, the both of us, with jobs, who paid rent. I lived with a woman, Emily. She was inside the apartment at the time, sleeping where adults usually sleep, in a bed. I had made it to our door and managed to fit the key in the lock before lying down and curling up on our welcome mat. This she read on the note you wrote, after you opened the door and dragged me inside to our living room couch, where she found me in the morning. You took my shoes off and left the keys and the note on the table in the foyer. Needless to say, this was all very kind of you. Thank you for not drawing on me or emptying my wallet.

I had been out at a bachelor party earlier that evening and vastly overserved by a string of irresponsible bartenders at a number of different establishments. The last thing I remember, and vaguely, is being at WXOU on Hudson Street a few blocks north of our building. I knew I was very drunk, apparently, as I've been told I turned to a friend and said, "I'm in big trouble," before stumbling to the door.

Sort of miraculous that I was able to make it as far as I did, I guess. The homing-pigeon autopilot part of the human brain is strong. But I can't imagine you were very impressed with me when you found me there. In fact, it was probably a bummer. Besides being an eyesore and a fire hazard, I became a situation to handle, heavy lifting to do upon coming home late yourself. I had food all over my clothes, too— there'd been a food fight over dinner. It's probably safe to assume we were not the most popular crew at the strip club.

We bumped into each other recently, you and I. Earlier this year at the Children's Museum in Brooklyn. I was there with Emily and our four-year-old son. You were pushing your own kid in a stroller. I walked up and said hello and reintroduced myself. We hadn't seen each other in the seven years since I moved out of the building on Morton Street. You were friendly and we compared the ages of our children and laughed about how different life was now. Then your wife walked up, and you said, "Hey, honey. This is Dave; he used to live next to me in the apartment on Morton Street."

"Ohh," she said, shaking my hand and breaking into a smile. "You're the guy we found in the hallway that night!"

I didn't even know she was there that night. I didn't know we'd ever met. She seemed lovely.

■ ■ ■

Dear Robert Sean Leonard,

I'm sorry if I freaked you out that morning you were walking your dog in front of the building where we lived in the West Village.

Our relationship had been fraught from the outset, I realize. When I first met you in the stairwell, the day I was moving in, and you were so friendly and welcoming, and I asked if we knew each other because you looked so familiar, and you said you didn't think so, I persisted, wondering if we'd perhaps gone to the same summer camp when we were kids, which forced you into the uncomfortable disclosure of the fact that you were a professional actor and "in some movies and on TV sometimes." A few days later, I saw you by the deli outside and greeted you by announcing that I'd remembered where I'd recognized you from. *"Dead Poets Society,* right?" You smiled graciously before I added, not being able to think of anything else, "You were good."

Still, you were always nice whenever we bumped into each other. So I feel even worse about that time that I corralled you by the front door to our building as the sun was coming up and you were taking your Chihuahua out for a walk. This was a few months before I got married. Emily—she's the woman I shared my apartment with; you might remember her giant head of curly blonde hair—and I were busy planning our wedding. The invitations were to go out that week, in fact. Planning a wedding is stressful, and I'd overrewarded myself for the previous day's work of finalizing the guest list, confirming mailing addresses, and was thus coming home at that time on a Wednesday morning, still full of the cocaine I'd been out all night doing.

Anyway, also that week, the musical *The Producers* had opened on Broadway to universal raves. And in my enthusiasm, and the difficulty I was having thinking straight, I congratulated you on the achievement. "Hey, way to go," I said. "Those were *some* reviews you got!"

You looked confused. And a little frightened. But you were as nice as ever in telling me you didn't know what I was talking about. "I guess I missed that one," you said, leaving open the possibility that, despite appearances, I was not in fact completely out of my mind. "I don't usually read the reviews."

I thought you were just being modest. "Oh, but these

weren't just any old reviews," I said. "You're in the hit of the city!"

You laughed nervously.

"Everybody's talking about it," I went on. "You must be totally psyched!"

You smiled politely and pretended that your dog was pulling harder on its leash than it was. Then you moved gingerly away from me.

I shrugged. "Have a good day," I said and went inside.

There, I found trouble because I had not called home earlier to tell Emily that I would be out so late. She had to get up for work in the morning, and I hadn't wanted to wake her. Also, I didn't have a cell phone. (I am a late adapter.)

I eased the door shut behind me, relocked the bolt with the quietest click I could manage, and tiptoed down the hall. But Emily was already awake, standing in the middle of the living room with the phone in her hand, looking differently than I'd ever seen her look before. Creases marked her forehead and the skin on her cheeks looked cracked. Salt. She'd been crying, though she wasn't anymore. Now her face was clenched rigid and she breathed hard through her nose.

"Hi," I said and felt myself smile dumbly at the confession.

She trembled, suppressing something, and her head twitched.

"You're up early," I said.

"Is this a test?" she said. Her voice was tight but her eyes were wild. "Is that what this is? A fucking test of my tolerance?" Then she shouted, "Is this what living together is?! Is this marriage?! Is this what it's going to be like?!"

"No." I had the sensation of slipping backward downhill. "Hold on…"

"Where *were* you?! I wake up at six o'clock in the fucking morning and you're not here, and I checked the machine and there's no message, and you won't get a fucking cell phone so I can call you! Fucking asshole! I don't know where you are or what you might be doing. I'm thinking you're dead or bleeding in a gutter somewhere. I was getting ready to start calling people. I didn't know where you were. I didn't know what to do." Her posture crumpled. She covered her eyes with her hand and sobbed. "I was scared," she said. "I was so worried!"

Her shoulders shook. Tears streamed down her cheeks. I couldn't talk. I wanted to say I was sorry. I wanted to tell her where I'd been, which was just at a bar and then my friend's apartment, and explain why I hadn't called. But a gulp broke in my throat and I swallowed dry air. I thought I was going to cry, too. I *wanted* to cry, to let her know how bad I felt for making her feel so bad. But I didn't cry. My tear ducts were empty. The coke, I suppose.

Emily had always been generously accepting of my lifestyle choices. I never had to hide anything from her. I'd had friends who had to lie and sneak around and use Binaca and Visine and stuff in order to keep their vices secret from their girlfriends and wives, and I never would have wanted to be in a relationship like that. We gave each other space, she and I. We didn't have to spend every moment together or insist that we take up each other's hobbies. It reminded me of that Kahlil Gibran poem people always read at weddings about how each individual string needs to quiver separately in order for a lute to make nice music, and how "the oak tree and the cypress grow not in each other's shadow." That had always made sense to me, and I took pride in how we didn't lose ourselves—our *selves*, our individuality—even as we'd decided to spend the rest of our lives together.

But that morning, how rotten I felt, taught me something about what it really means to spend your life with someone, about committing to that. I had always believed that as long as a person wasn't acting out of malice, he or she couldn't really be blamed for the way anyone felt about it. People are responsible for their own feelings. But here I had hurt the person I would have least wanted to hurt in the world. Out of carelessness, not malice—in fact, part of it was out of consideration, the not wanting to wake her up. (Well, consideration combined with addle-brained stupidity.) And I could see why she was hurt. Emily had invested her future in me; she had a right to care more about me, and a right to expect more care in return, and more consideration of her care, than I gave to other people. Benign intentions were not enough. My behavior carried ramifications for her. If my string was out of tune—too tight, too high, or too loose and unfocused—it would fuck up her song.

I found my voice after a moment and apologized as best as I could. I went to her and put my arms around her and told her over and over again how sorry I was, how much I loved her, that I would try my very best to never scare her like that again. She calmed down and took a shower and went to work. I went to bed angry at myself, thinking about change.

After I woke up, halfway through the afternoon, I remembered that you were not in *The Producers*. That was Matthew Broderick.

ADULTHOOD

(Or in my thirties, approaching middle age, but more often than I would wish, still doing things that leave me feeling like a goofy twelve-year-old.)

Dear Cousins from Israel,

I'm sorry for not talking to you at my wedding.

I will feel like a schmuck about this forever. You took me on a cross-country van trip when I was seven, still the only time I've seen the Grand Canyon and Mount Rushmore and Joshua Tree. You put me up at your house in Israel over three summers, when I was ten, when I was eleven, when I was twenty-two. And you traveled so far. A twelve-hour flight!

Emily and I were surprised, we didn't think you'd come. We were surprised by a lot of things about the wedding. For a long time, we didn't think we would even have one. We were originally opposed to the institution of marriage for the same reasons that so many people develop as young adults: smash the patriarchy, etc. Even after we'd figured out that we wanted to spend the rest of our lives together, when we started talking about getting married, the legal and tax-code advantages, we thought we might elope, just have a small civil ceremony at city hall, and tell everybody after the fact. Upon further discussion, though, knowing how much it would mean to our families, we opted to make it an event.

Not that we felt that the patriarchy didn't still deserve to be smashed. We resolved to avoid any fuddy-duddy formality. We'd both been to weddings that seemed more like a trial than a celebration. Ours, we said, would be a party, first and foremost—short on ceremony, long on lobster and Pimm's Cups and Frisbee and hip-hop. We promised each other that we would have fun. In retrospect, this is to say that we went into the endeavor under false, or at least contradictory, pretenses. In agreement that the wedding was more for other people than for us, we proceeded to talk ourselves into a mutually reinforced sense of entitlement. (We wanted to have our cake because we knew our moms wanted us to have our cake, but we wanted to eat it, the whole cake, by ourselves, too. To torture a particularly fitting figure of speech.)

I will give myself a partial break and acknowledge that a wedding is an endeavor that naturally leads to this kind of selfishness. In choosing to get married, in the announcement and the planning and the whirlwind months of preparation, two people are susceptible to falling into a circle-the-wagons, it's-you-and-me-against-the-world mind-set. Having declared Emily to be my favorite person in the world, having established her as my priority, it was all too easy to push everything and everyone else to the periphery of my attention. Love has tunnel vision.

So, wrapped up in myself even more than I usually am, I was not noticing a lot at the time. Most dramatically, I didn't notice my sister Debby's weight loss in the months leading up to the wedding. She was living in New York then, working for an educational nonprofit on lower Broadway, so I was seeing her regularly. We'd meet for lunch or go jogging to-

gether by the river. She'd throw dinner parties that would end with this amazing apple-walnut cake she'd invented. But I guess in the way they say a frog will let itself be boiled alive in a pot of water if the temperature is raised incrementally, I didn't notice how really much too thin she was getting. I remember telling her she looked great—a memory that hits me in the stomach even as I type it now, and even harder when I look at the pictures of Deb from the wedding. The way her collarbone jutted out from below her neck, the sharpness of her shoulder blades. Parts of my sister's skeleton we had never seen before.

She had long impressed everyone who'd met her with her maturity. And it was impressive: she had a gravitas beyond her age. She had her act together in ways that I'd never had. She'd come up to visit me at college once and we went to a party at a house off campus and people asked who was older. (I am *seven years* older.)

It was understandable: after our dad died, she grew up fast. She got an older boyfriend—one who unfortunately developed an addiction to heroin. She graduated high school a year early and spent a year living in Colorado before starting college at Connecticut College, where I had gone. Then, during Christmas break her freshman year, soon after she'd broken up with her heroin-addicted boyfriend once and for all, he told her, over the phone, "I hope you sleep well at night," and shot himself with his father's gun. I will never forget the sound of her voice when I called home to talk to her. She wailed like a wounded animal.

Even after that, though, even after enduring that second major, horrible trauma before her eighteenth birthday, she recovered and seemed great—bright and bubbly and extraordinarily capable. She had good friends and graduated college in four years (always a monumental accomplishment, from my perspective) and moved to New York and got this cool job at a cool office and was promoted twice in her first year there. She was running after-school arts programs at forty city schools. Times I would come to pick her up at work, her colleagues raved about her to me when she was out of earshot. She was a world-beater, people said.

I didn't realize anything was wrong until the night before the wedding. We were at Emily's folks' place in upstate New York, where we'd decided to hold the event. Many of us had crammed into the small house: Emily and I; her parents; her sister Lucy and Lucy's boyfriend, Matt; and Deb. I woke up around three o'clock in the morning and went to pee and heard typing coming from the living room, where Deb was sleeping on an inflatable mattress. I walked out there to find her hunched over her laptop, computer-blue light on her face in the otherwise dark room.

"What are you doing?" I asked.

"Ughhh!" she turned to me, surprised—and more stressed out and frantic looking than anyone should be at three o'clock in the morning. "I'm working on my toast."

"Oh, man, don't worry about it. It'll be fine, whatever you say. Or don't give one if you don't want to. You don't have to."

She said that Lucy had written something so she had to, too. She seemed sad, her face so drawn.

"Get some sleep," I said.

"I just want it to be good," she said, turning back to the screen.

I myself had not been feeling stressed out in the days before the wedding. After a week of rain that had had Emily's mom in a tizzy, we'd been blessed with four days of blue skies. Everything had come together nicely—the tent was up, the Porta-Potties in place, our fishmonger, Darryl, on his way from the docks of Boston. (This thanks to my in-laws, as they did the on-site organizing.) It would be a big party, the biggest either of us had ever thrown surely, 125 people, but it was just a party. My feet were a very comfortable temperature. It would be fun.

The morning of June 9, 2001, we ran electrical cords to a circle Em's father had cleared among the pine trees in the woods and helped my friends Todd and Mike set up their instruments—two guitars, one acoustic, one pedal steel. I had asked them to play something soft and pretty. (And as a cheesy in-joke for anyone who grew up listening to classic-rock radio, Eric Clapton's "Wonderful Tonight.") And we practiced where we'd walk and where we'd stand for the ceremony.

Guests began arriving early in the afternoon. Greeting the first of them at tables of food and drink set up on the sloping lawn above the house, I found the nervousness I'd been so happily spared to that point. Introducing a college friend and his wife to a work friend and her date, I forgot the name of my college friend's wife—a woman I had met numerous times, a woman whose wedding I'd attended. I stammered and waited for my friend to bail me out, and he did, but then I looked over his shoulder, down the hill, and saw a thick stream of people marching up the driveway. They were all coming to see Emily and me; I would have to introduce so many of them to each other. I felt the pair of raw oysters I'd eaten swimming around in the Pimm's Cup I had drunk. It felt like they were doing unsynchronized somersaults.

So I didn't eat or drink anything else, and I survived the next hour and a half by letting people introduce themselves to one another. There were so many people—the yard was like a *Sgt. Pepper's* cover full of familiar faces: friends from childhood, high school, college, work; my mom's family from Rochester and Missouri; Ava and Lewis from Boston; Josh from Michigan; and you guys, all the way from Israel. A collage of my first thirty years on the planet.

Once everybody had had a chance to arrive and have a few oysters and drinks, Debby and Lucy led a procession into the woods. Emily and I waited for five minutes, and then we took each other's hands and followed. Everyone was smiling as we walked down the aisle. Todd and Mike sounded perfect—the pedal steel notes pealing in the sunlight that filtered through the tops of the pine trees. People who recognized *Wonderful Tonight* chuckled. The air smelled good.

Our friends Dave and Georgia, whom we'd asked to conduct the ceremony, stood up in front of everybody and said things that made me cry a little bit. Then Emily and I read the vows we'd written and exchanged our rings and slipped them on our fingers and kissed, and everybody clapped and cheered. The next twelve hours are a swirling blur in my memory, punctuated by moments of transcendent, euphoric clarity: The crack of the shell, the splatter and steam, as I snapped the tail off my lobster. Gazing out from under the eaves of the tent, seeing the sky turn violet over a Wiffle Ball game as the sun set—the deep contentment, the pride, I guess, that I felt when I saw how many people were playing, twenty or so, and how many of them had never met before that day. Dancing with Emily as Stevie Wonder sang about love lasting until the rainbow burns the stars out in the sky and stretched the word *always* longer than thirty syllables in the explosion of pure joy at the end of "As." (On the record that our DJ, Chris, was spinning, I mean. Stevie Wonder did not perfrom live at our wedding.)

Some wise person had advised Emily and me to take half an hour to walk off by ourselves at some point during the festivities—a moment to breathe and enjoy one another's company amid the craziness of the day. We sat on a bench near the stone wall that bordered the woods and felt happier than either of us had ever thought we would ever feel.

But we should have also done something that we'd seen other brides and grooms do at other weddings—we should have taken a half an hour to walk around to each table during the meal and say hello to everybody and thank them for coming. We didn't. By design; the couples we'd seen do this never looked happy while they were doing it, stiff smiles, forced small talk, laden with obligation. It was like a receiving line, which has always seemed like the worst kind of torture to me. Considering it further, it is exactly like that. It is in lieu of standing on a receiving line that couples do the walk around the dinner tables. But I now see the value, the reason for the practice. A few short minutes of thinking about people other than myself. Even if it would have been a slight discomfort, less than a hundred percent fun, would it not have been worth a few short minutes to let people—you, in particular—know how much I appreciated their coming to celebrate the day with me? How much it meant to me to have everyone there? Rather than just basking in all the love I was being showered with? Like some kind of rock star onstage? Like Sting, closing his eyes and spreading his arms out in that Jaguar commercial that made me wish I could throw something at him through my television screen. That was me that day, like fucking Sting. Yes, it would have been worth it. It would have been worth anything to not be like Sting.

Debby struggled with her emotions during her toast. She said lots of nice things, but she had written too much. Feeling the minutes in front of an audience, she flipped past pages she was holding in her hands. She started crying when she mentioned that she knew that my father would have loved Emily and had trouble regaining her composure.

My mom, always thoughtful, devoted her toast to you and all the other relatives, thanking you for traveling and mentioning you each by name. But it was not enough, I'm afraid, to cover my rudeness. Did I even say hello to you? Give a hug and a kiss? I'd like to think so. I know I saw you. But I worry that I didn't say more than that. I know I didn't say very much more.

The day after the wedding, Emily and I got into a rental car to drive to the airport to fly to Italy for our honeymoon. As we pulled out of the driveway, our remaining friends and family waving to us in the rearview mirror, I turned and said, "I'm worried about my sister. I don't think she's doing too good."

"Clearly," Emily said, agreeing more quickly than I'd expected. "She's lost much too much weight much too fast. She has an eating disorder."

That had not occurred to me before, but it was true. Deb had a long struggle ahead of her. She's doing better now.

Luckily for us, you guys are avid travelers. Emily and I have had other opportunities to spend time with you. You are exceptionally enjoyable people to spend time with. Family is something that I have taken for granted too much in my life, too often paid too little mind. Having made the choice to marry, and now with a young child of my own, I see importance in things that I could not before. I need to be more attentive.

■ ■ ■

DAVE BRY

Dear Seventy-Year-Old Man in a Leg Brace,

I'm sorry for not being able to change a tire on my own car.

It was hot that day, late summer 2003, on that desert highway in Wyoming, an hour or two outside of Cheyenne. And it was a rental car, actually, the convertible Mustang my wife and I were standing next to when you pulled onto the shoulder and parked behind us. Did that car look fast? It was. Could it go 130 miles per hour on a straightaway? It could. Should I have pushed it to that speed? I should not have.

The car had started to clunk and jerk a few miles back. We were down in the double digits by that time. (Thank god. I'm sure we would have burst into flames had anything happened at a buck thirty.) I'd kept going for a while, hoping to make it to a gas station, but it quickly became clear we were riding on the rim. I pulled off the road, stopped the car, and got out.

We were on vacation, driving the vast open spaces of the American West. The Rockies, Yellowstone, Devil's Tower. (That's the big rock from *Close Encounters of the Third Kind*, as I'm sure you know.) It's beautiful country. But I've never felt more like Woody Allen, standing there frowning at that shredded tire—out of cell-phone service range, tumbleweed and cattle skulls littering the sunbaked landscape, vultures circling in the sky above. (Were there in fact vultures? I think there were.) I didn't know what to do. There's a reason I live in New York. I can barely change the filter in our humidifier.

I'd read somewhere that it's safe to drink one's own urine for up to seven cycles in a dehydrative emergency. Still, we were very happy when we saw your pickup coming toward us on the road.

Getting a first look at you through your windshield, I figured you'd drive us to an auto shop in the nearest town—or that you'd have a CB radio and could call a tow truck for help before mountain lions and coyotes came to eat us. You were small and wizened, and I certainly would not have expected you to be able to fix a broken car. You asked what the problem was and I told you we had a flat tire, and you asked me if I needed something called a jack. I was embarrassed to tell you that I didn't know what that word meant. I was more embarrassed when you opened your door, swung out your left leg, which was encased in some sort of medical brace with bolts and metal hinges, hopped down from your seat, and hobbled your way over to the Mustang.

I heard my father's voice in my memory. I'd always been mechanically disinclined. He used to tell me that I should at least learn the basics of auto repair, if only for instances such as this. "You shouldn't be driving if you don't have at least a little understanding of how a car's engine works," he said. He bought me *Zen and the Art of Motorcycle Maintenance* when I was a teenager. But I never read it.

It's no great Freudian leap to imagine that I resisted proficiency in this area precisely because it was important to my dad that I achieve it. That I kept myself so ignorant and incompetent as a sort of rebellion, in defiance of a standard of masculinity that I felt he had tried to push on me. I could accept that that might be the case, even if it was largely subconscious. (Although it could very well just be that I don't have the head for it, that I was born without the acumen. I can't follow directions to assemble my kid's Lego sets, either. I start to hyperventilate at the first sentence of any instruction manual. It feels like the letters of the words are falling off the page, like when Sylvia Plath has her first mental breakdown in the *Bell Jar*. Did you read that one?)

Under the rug in my trunk, as you showed me, there was a clever hidden compartment containing a spare tire, an X-shaped tool, and, lo and behold, a jack—which turned out to be an accordion-like mechanism with which a seventy-year-old man in a leg brace can lift two thousand pounds of metal off the ground. Magic, in other words.

My kid will probably grow up to be an underwater welder for oil rigs in the Gulf of Mexico. I would be happy for that. (Well, I mean, except for the danger, the explosions, and sharks and stuff.) I would be happy if he didn't find himself in situations where he felt helpless and out of his element. I would like him to feel more of a sense of mastery over the physical world than I do, more comfortable with machines and technology.

Before I could figure out something to say or do that might have been in any way useful, you dropped to the ground, flipped over on your back, and slid yourself under the back of my car. "*I should really be doing this part,*" I whispered to Emily, who nodded, as you disappeared. But then, I had no idea what you were looking for. I watched the brace drag tracks in the sand and imagined how uncomfortable it must have been to have such a thing strapped over your dusty blue jeans in this heat. I was wearing shorts and flip-flops.

But everyone feels helpless and out of his or her element sometimes. No one can master everything. I remember the look on my father's face one day when a trailer he'd hitched to our car came unbolted on the road. Part of his horror was the surprise—the failure of an expertise he'd trusted in himself. I wish he could have been spared the feelings that that look betrayed. Might a bumbling incompetent like myself have an easier time handling those moments when life spins out of control? If only for having more practice? That's an argument for irresponsibility, I realize—and craven; a beta wolf living off another's hunting. And if followed to its conclusion and applied across the spectrum, one that would lead to a smaller, sadder world.

Once you'd found the right place to put the jack, you cranked up the chassis and had the new tire on and road ready in a matter of minutes. You let me spin the X-shaped wrench a couple times, more for the sake of humoring me, it seemed, than anything else.

There must be a happy medium. I hope my kid can tackle tasks at which I throw up my hands, only to tell self-deprecating stories about later. But I hope he doesn't judge himself too harshly when he fails.

You didn't say much. Just smiled and nodded when I thanked you a hundred times. And refused to take any of the money I offered for your trouble. You were like a cowboy hero come to life, like the Lone Ranger. I was so lame.

■ ■ ■

Dear Stephen Malkmus,

Sorry if I came off like a stalker when I told you that I'd named my child after one of your songs.

It was strangely warm the day we met in fall of 2005. I was wearing a sweatshirt and sweating in it as I stood at the corner of Houston Street and Avenue A with a heavy bag of groceries in each hand. You walked up pushing a baby stroller and waited there, five feet away, for the crosswalk sign to change. I got a giddy rush when I saw you. You are one of my all-time favorite rock 'n' roll heroes.

Not that I hadn't seen you in person before. I worked at a music magazine, and my roommate from college used to help put on those Tibetan Freedom Concerts you used to take part in. I interviewed your bandmates Scott Kannberg and Steve West once while you sat at the next table over, being interviewed by Lynn Hirschberg for *Rolling Stone*. And I'd seen you backstage at the concerts and at parties and stuff. Most recently, I'd seen you in my local coffee shop. Full City, the place was called, right across the street from the building where I lived on the Lower East Side. Full City got their coffee beans from a place in Portland, Oregon, according to a sign by the counter. You lived in Portland, I knew, so at first I wondered whether you were particular enough about your coffee to have found the one place in New York that carried your preferred product when you were in town for work. But then Natalie, the proprietor of Full City, told me you'd in fact moved to New York, to the neighborhood—you'd moved in with your girlfriend, who lived right down the block.

I didn't know you had a kid, though. I was surprised to see the stroller. This was maybe why I decided to say hello when I hadn't the other times. I don't usually approach a famous person when I see one on the street. I figure people don't want to be bothered. But I was a new father myself at the time; my son had been born ten months earlier. We were standing right next to each other. It almost felt weird *not* to say something.

"Excuse me, Stephen?" I said, turning toward you. "Hi. My name's Dave. I just wanted to tell you how much your music's meant to me. It's meant a lot."

"Oh, thanks," you said in the same slack, slightly off-kilter voice I knew from listening to your records a gazillion times.

"That's all," I said, starting to turn back away. "I just wanted to say hello."

"So, what's up?" You smiled and shrugged and sounded friendly. Friendlier than I'd expected.

I was taken off guard. You wanted to talk to me?

"Oh. Umm." I was extremely psyched. But I didn't have anything else to say. "I don't know." I nodded down to the bags I was carrying. "Doing some shopping."

The light changed. You nodded south and asked if I was going that way. I was. We crossed Houston and started walking down Essex Street together. You asked where I lived and I told you and you told me you'd just moved into the neighborhood. I didn't say, "Yeah, I heard that," because I thought that might be weird, but I did tell you that I'd seen you at the Full City coffee shop a couple times. "Oh yeah," you said. "They have good coffee there."

My sweatshirt was much too warm and zipped up, and I couldn't unzip it or wipe the sweat off my forehead because my hands were full of the very heavy grocery bags. I was sweating a lot. It was like Albert Brooks in *Broadcast News*. But if you noticed, you didn't say anything. We talked about local real estate, which is about the most boring thing you can talk about, but was about the coolest thing I could imagine that day. Me and Stephen Malkmus, boring, local-real-estate-interested thirty-somethings—together! I cited a statistic I'd read recently and you said you'd read that, too. "We must have read the same article," you said. I suppressed a teenybopper's giggle.

We passed Stanton Street and came to Rivington. You were turning east. I turned, too. I could've kept going south and turned later; I didn't have a set route. But I did eventually need to turn east. I was enjoying the conversation. Were you? I doubt that you were enjoying it as much as I was. That would've been hard to imagine. But you didn't seem to be *not* enjoying it. So I turned with you. After a couple more steps, I looked down into the stroller you were pushing and saw a baby girl. "What's her name?" I asked. You told me and I said that was nice. (It was.) I asked how old she was, and when you told me, I said that I had a little boy around that age at home. We exchanged congratulations and then condolences, agreeing that the difficulty of this first year would mean that our children would be only children.

"What's your little guy's name?" you asked.

Sweat streamed down past my ear onto my neck. "Well, it's kind of funny," I said, and coughed a laugh in confession. "Because it's actually a name that I know mostly from one of your songs." I told you my kid's name and you said, "Oh yeah," and recited the line from the song. This felt very weird to me, like parts of my life were coming together in ways I never thought they would, and I wondered how it felt to you. I wondered whether you were regretting your decision to strike up the conversation or that you'd told me where you lived and your daughter's name.

"We really just liked the way it sounds," I said, hoping that might reassure you.

You seemed unbothered. "I've always liked that name," you said. "I've always associated it with the Old South for some reason."

We walked and talked past Norfolk and Suffolk Streets. You were nothing but nice the whole time. But when we came to the corner of Rivington and Clinton, you nodded to Caffe Falai. "We're gonna stop in there," you said. "Okay," I said. I decided not to stop with you.

"What did you say your name was again?" you asked.

"Dave," I said. You smiled a small, half-embarrassed smile and you indicated yourself. "Steve," you said, shrugging again. You were just being polite. You knew I knew your name.

You've since moved away. Back to Portland with the family. I just learned you did wind up having a second kid. So congratulations and condolences again. I never saw you at Full City anymore after that day. I sort of wonder why. I sort of have a hunch.

■ ■ ■

Dear Step-Nephew,

I'm sorry for cursing at you at Thanksgiving at our aunt's house.

November 2005. You were fifteen at the time or sixteen. Regardless, I used words that were very inappropriate for me to use in that situation. I was thirty-four.

We were in the kitchen at our mutual aunt's house in Boston. I'd just arrived, after a long drive with my wife and not-quite-one-year-old kid and my mother. You and your folks had gotten there the day before. We were both up from New York, but I hadn't seen you in a few years. Not since you were much shorter and much less opinionated about the city's neighborhoods and socioeconomic matters. Or at least less colorful in the expression of your opinions.

We were catching up, making the sort of small talk I thought pretty normal for a pair of extended family members who only see each other every few years at Thanksgiving.

"So you're in high school now," I said. "Cool."

"I see you've grown your hair long," I said. "Cool."

"Oh, you play guitar?"

I probably used the word *cool* too much. And you probably thought I was trying too hard to *relate* or whatever. I don't often talk to teenagers these days. But I remember being one. And I was enjoying how fully you lived up to type. The bored, weary tone of voice, the skull with snakes coming out its eyes on your T-shirt, the put-upon half sneer in which you held your upper lip. You were totally awesome.

And, I'm sure, totally miserable. Trapped in Boston with your parents for four days instead of smoking pot with your friends and masturbating in the privacy of your own bathroom. I know I would have been.

I asked where in New York you lived and you told me Brooklyn and a neighborhood I can't recall. Then I was taken aback when—after you asked me the same question and I told you that we had moved to the Lower East Side of Manhattan—that sneer curled a bit higher and you called me "fucking bourgeois scum."

I'm not sure exactly what the appropriate response would have been. Maybe a more responsible adult would have gone and told your parents. Perhaps, in times past, someone in my position would have simply smacked you across the face or marched you over to the sink and washed your mouth out with soap. But thinking back on it, it was less the language that offended me than it was the accusation. Bourgeois?! Me?! *(Moi?!)* I saw Jane's Addiction headline Lollapalooza in 1991! I guess I thought (without really thinking, of course—again, it had been a long drive) that cursing back at you would send a message. My knee-jerk intent was to shock you, to prove that I wasn't too old, or too stodgy, or too bourgeois to use bad words.

I know better now. You were at a difficult age. And "suck my dick, you little punk" is really never the right thing to say to one's nephew. Especially at Thanksgiving.

■ ■ ■

Dear Rory's Parents,

I'm sorry if I conjured a disturbing image for you at Jack's birthday party.

It was a few years ago now that we found ourselves talking by the bowl of ranch dressing dip. Jack was turning four. I was there because my kid was in Jack's preschool class. You're friends with Jack's parents, I believe. One of you works with one of them or something. Anyway, you have a son who was at the party, too. Rory.

Being that four-year-old birthday parties are geared for the entertainment of four-year-olds, they're generally not so much fun for grown-ups. Even less so when the birthday boy is a classmate of your kid's, as opposed to, say, the kid of one of your friends. I didn't know any of the adults who were there very well. Still, even though I would have rather been sitting in the corner with headphones on, watching the episode of *Star Wars: The Clone Wars* that was being projected on the wall, I made an effort to have a conversation.

"Rory's a nice name," I said. "It's Scottish, right?"

You didn't know. Neither one of you are Scottish, it turns out. You just liked the sound of it. You asked me if I was Scottish. I said no but that I always thought of Rory as a Scottish name because I knew it mostly from a song by a Scottish band I like. I should have stopped talking right before I said that, but I didn't. "The Vaselines," I said. "Do you guys know them?" You didn't. I didn't expect you to. They're kind of obscure. "They sing that song 'Jesus Doesn't Want Me for a Sunbeam' that Nirvana played on the *MTV Unplugged* thing." You did know that song, you said.

"What's the song with Rory in it?" one of you asked, perfectly friendly.

That was when I knew I should have stopped talking earlier.

"Oh," I said, feeling the pores in the skin on the top of my head open up. "It's actually, umm, in the title to the song."

You waited.

I should have lied. How hard would it have been to make up a song title with Rory in it? "Rory Be Mine." "Hey, Hey, Rory." "Rory Wants a New Pair of Shoes." Whatever.

Instead, I gritted my teeth and, in the most casual, least

creepy voice I could manage, told the truth. "Rory Rides Me Raw," I said.

I could tell from the looks on your faces that you hadn't heard of that one.

We didn't talk much more after that, though the party was a long one. They waited for the balloon-tying clown to show up before serving the cake. It felt like forever.

■ ■ ■

Dear Night Shift Manager at the Sheridan Garage,

Sorry for taking the key out of the engine of my car after you jumped the battery.

This was on July 12, 2010, after a series of events that left me frazzled but also counting my lucky stars. My wife, Emily, and I were driving home from a weekend at her parents' place upstate. Our five-year-old son was asleep in the backseat. Around ten o'clock, somewhere on the Taconic Parkway in Westchester, an orange light reading "ABS" appeared on the dashboard display. I had no idea what this meant. (A message from god to start working out?) But when I pointed it out to Emily, she guessed it stood for antilock braking system. I don't know how she knew this—Emily grew up in New York City and doesn't drive—but she was right. Still, neither of us knew what we should do about it. The car seemed to be driving fine, so I figured I'd just look into it after we got home.

A little while later, after the Taconic had turned into the Sprain, I noticed that all the other dashboard lights seemed to be dimming. At least, I thought this was the case. I wasn't sure. I wondered whether it was just that they *looked* dimmer in comparison to the brighter orange ABS light that was new to the scene. I was still wondering about this as the Sprain turned into the Bronx River Parkway and when the little red picture of the battery lit up. Also, we seemed to be losing our headlights. But again, it was hard to be sure because of the brake lights on the car ahead of us.

"This is bad," I said to Emily. But I couldn't figure out why the battery would be dying while the car was driving. I thought that just happened when you left the car parked overnight with the lights on. I don't know very much about how cars work. In fact, I know so little about how cars work that I'd be sympathetic to the argument that I should not ever drive one again. Well, at least, that's how I felt at the end of that night.

"I guess we need a new battery?" I said. But we still didn't know what to do. I didn't know how long it took for a battery to die after the warning light went on. "I hope we make it home." I turned off the radio and the air-conditioning. There were lots of other cars around us, driving fast on the confusing sprawl of highways and bridges and exits and merges that circles the city. The shoulder looked thin and uninviting, especially with the kid in the backseat.

It turns out it doesn't take very long for the battery to die after the warning light goes on. We got off the parkway at the 177th Street exit and went under the Cross Bronx onto the Sheridan Expressway. And then the engine started slowing down. I pressed hard on the gas pedal and the car started herky-jerking. We were in the middle lane. Cars zoomed past on either side of us. I pushed the button for the hazard lights, but they didn't go on.

I said, "Fuck," and asked Emily to unroll her window to signal to the cars around us. Her window rolled down three inches and stopped. "It won't go down," she said.

The worst part of our night came when I saw in the rearview mirror that there was an eighteen-wheeler truck merging onto the road behind us. Merging into the right lane, where I was at the time trying to aim the lurching, sputtering, largely invisible, electronically sealed death box that contained my family. I held my breath and let it pass and then cut off another car to turn into the right lane. Then, thank god, we found ourselves on an exit ramp. It was an upward incline, which was not great. But it was straight, which was great, because I now noticed that the steering wheel was resisting my turning it.

The best part of our night came when Emily saw a sign for the Sheridan Garage across the street from the top of the ramp. I pulled into the parking lot and felt the steering wheel freeze into a locked position just as we rolled through the open door and under the fluorescent lights. "Wow." I stopped the car and turned to Emily. "That was really lucky!"

This is perhaps where the worst part of your night began. You work at the Sheridan Garage. And after I got out of my car and knocked on the frosted-glass kiosk there, it was you who opened the door and stepped out to greet me.

You were nothing but nice. But we had trouble communicating because you don't speak very much English and I don't speak very much Spanish. At first, you thought I just wanted to park my car at the garage. But I was able to express the truth of the situation by pointing to the car and saying, "Battery," and making a knife out of fingers and drawing it across my throat. You perked up and said the word *jump* and called out, "JoJo!" and some words in Spanish. I smiled and shrugged. Could it be that all the car needed was to have its battery jumped? Seemed unlikely. But what did I know? I wished I could have admitted to you my level of ignorance about cars from the outset.

JoJo, a younger man in a blue polo shirt, appeared from the back of the garage pulling a dolly. On the dolly was a milk crate that held a car battery with jumper cables attached. You asked me to open the hood and I did, and you connected the cables and told me to start the car, and I tried to but it wouldn't start. You talked to JoJo and unconnected the cables and reconnected them in a few different places, one of which resulted in sparks and, apparently, a shock to your hand. But after some more discussion with JoJo and a couple more tries, the car finally started up. You smiled proudly and gave me a conclusive nod. JoJo unconnected the cables and put them back into the milk crate and carted the jumper battery away. But the car didn't sound so good, and I saw that the ABS light and the little red battery were once again lit up on the dashboard. I got out of the car and brought this to your attention. You got into the driver's seat and inspected the dashboard and revved the engine, which sputtered. "No good," you said. "Yeah," I said.

You said something in Spanish and I shrugged. You said a word that sounded like *alternator* and got out of the car and pointed to a part of the engine that Internet research has since told me is called the alternator. "Oh," I said, nodding stupidly. "That's it." We then spent a couple minutes coming to the understanding that there was a mechanic who worked at the garage who could fix the car and that I would come pick it up on Tuesday morning. You went back into the kiosk to call a taxi for us, and Emily went to wake up the kid. I got back into the car and took the keys out of the ignition so I could open the trunk to get our bags. This was a mistake.

You stuck your head back out of the kiosk when you heard the engine stop running. "No," you said, looking at me standing next to the car with the keys in my hand. "No off!"

"Oooh," I said, realizing that you would need to move the car out of the entranceway to the garage.

"No off! Aye, papi, no off!" You shook your head sadly and started walking to the back of the garage. "JoJo!"

Sorry about that.

■ ■ ■

PUBLIC APOLOGY

Dear Asa,

Sorry for letting you get lost in Prospect Park.

It was only for ten minutes. Nothing too terrible. But certainly no fun for anyone involved. You are my son, and this happened when you were five years old.

We had taken the train into Brooklyn on a Sunday and walked to Prospect Park with our friends Dave and Magda and their boys, Max, Zach, and Haig. We'd brought a small vinegar-and-baking-soda-fueled rocket that Dave had bought, and you guys were all very excited to try it out—running and jumping and picking up sticks, as boys will do in a park. You were the youngest but keeping up with the others just fine, and it felt like a very standard level of chaos as we turned off the path and into the great lawn to find a place to sit down and spread out a blanket at an open enough spot to make a launching pad. I don't know if you had raced ahead for a moment or dawdled behind, but you didn't turn with us, and we'd gotten out into the center of the grass before realizing that none of us, parents or the other boys, knew where you were.

I was calm for the first couple minutes. I went back to the path and retraced our steps to the pedestrian tunnel we'd come through, where a group of stoner teenagers were playing four square. You weren't there, so I went back to the lawn. It was crowded, a sea of taller bodies to wander among. How far could you have gotten? How long before you'd realize we weren't nearby? Would you remember the advice we'd given you, to stop walking in such a situation, to stay put and wait till we found you? I didn't know. I passed your mother, who had gone searching in another direction. "Fuck," she said, frowning and not joking while neither of us stopped. "We lost our kid."

I headed off on another angle through the lawn; she returned to the original path we'd come on and took it farther into the park. By the time I wound up back at the tunnel for a second time, my heart was beating hard in my chest. I envisioned you wandering into the darkness by yourself. I envisioned worse: a stranger snatching you, a large hand clamping over your small mouth.

I was consciously reminding myself not to panic, repeating the specific words in my head, *Don't panic, don't panic*, when I doubled back a second time. I saw Dave and Magda from a distance. They were standing where we'd first stopped, still scanning the crowd. I saw their boys running around, looking for you, trying to help. I felt my shoulders tightening as I walked. I couldn't go fast enough, couldn't cover enough ground. At what point do I start running? At what point do I start shouting your name? At what point should I call the cops? I felt dizzy for a second and told myself again to stay calm.

Parenthood is such a paradox. At the age of five, you were a lot like most five-year-old boys, which is to say, a constant stream of whining for ice cream, proclamations of your own superpowers, and scatological jokes that were not as funny to me as they were to you. You were high in pitch, volume, and energy, and desirous, to put it very mildly, of attention. There were plenty of times when your mother and I would have paid money for ten minutes of not being able to hear or see you. I think about those times, and then I think about the empty space I felt in my stomach that Sunday, how my heartbeat quickened and respiration became more difficult with every minute that we couldn't find you, and nothing in the world made any sense.

I know it won't ever end, either. I think about what I put my parents through when I was a teenager. What you'll surely put me through when you're a teenager.

It's a particular sort of guilt, a very strong strain, that comes from fucking up in terms of taking care of your kid. When I try to put my futile words to the experience of seeing you for the first time, laid out on the silver tray of the scale in the delivery room, moments after you were born, they pretty quickly come to the idea of protection. Right after the mind-blowing realization that you, this small breathing creature with eyelids and fingers, were in fact made out of parts of *me*, and the weird, almost physical feeling of connection that rose in my chest because of that, came the similarly mind-blowing understanding that I would step in front of a bus to push you out of the way. That I would choose to die so that you could live. I am a pretty self-centered person. I would maybe like to *think* that I would be willing to make such a sacrifice for your mom; or my sister, Debby; or say, a boatful of other people's children; or, in some sort of sci-fi scenario like Bruce Willis in *Armageddon*, the future of mankind itself. But I'd never really *known* the feeling before. The sureness of it, the *without a moment's thought.* I felt a compulsion, a brand-new gnawing inside, to put myself between you and danger. Even there, with the doctors standing next to me in the sterile confines of the delivery room, I checked the scale for sharp edges.

So a lapse in this regard, out of stupidity or absentmindedness, guilt almost doesn't describe it. It's more like a feeling of essential worthlessness: I have one job to do on this planet really, one simple mandate that comes before everything else, and I can't even get that right.

Finally, thank god, before I set off searching the whole of Prospect Park, before I broke into a trot or started screaming for help, my friend Dave waved across the field and gave me a thumbs-up. Zach, his middle son, was running toward him, shouting the news. Your mom had found you. You had indeed followed the path farther, a hundred yards or so past where we'd turned. You were near a big tree, walking in small circles and crying when she saw you. She had picked you up by the time I got there. Your face was all red and splotchy, and you still hadn't caught your breath.

I took you out of your mom's arms and hugged you tighter than usual. "We were so worried," I said, trying not to let you hear my voice crack. "We didn't know where you were."

ACKNOWLEDGMENTS

First thanks go to Choire Sicha and Alex Balk, who started my favorite website, The Awl, three years ago and let me write for it. Many of the apologies in this book were first published on The Awl. Choire and Balk are both excellent writers and editors, and I have learned a lot from them.

Here are other people who have taught me things about writing that I think ended up in this book: Elizabeth Wardell, Emma Betta, Blanche McCrary Boyd, Danyel Smith, Carter Harris.

I make some fun out of my less-than-valedictory collegiate record in this book, but I would like to thank Professor Larry Vogel and his colleagues in the Connecticut College Philosophy Department: Kristin Pfefferkorn-Forbath, Lester Reiss, Melvin Woody. They taught me things about thinking that I think ended up in this book.

Ann and James Raimes, and Matt Szenher and Lucy Raimes provided me with good, quiet places to write parts of this book.

ACKNOWLEDGMENTS

Kate Lee helped me turn a website column into a book and then sold it to Helen Atsma at Grand Central Publishing. Helen edited the book, and it is much, much better than it would have been otherwise. Kirsten Reach, Carolyn Kurek, and Heather Schroder provided invaluable assistance in making the book a book, too. Caitlin Mulrooney-Lyski helped sell it to you.

My friend Sara Vilkomerson introduced me to Choire and The Awl.

Emily Raimes and Asa Raimes Bry are the innermost core of my heart.

ABOUT THE AUTHOR

DAVE BRY has written for *Vibe*, *XXL* magazine, *Spin*, The Awl, and True/Slant. He lives in Brooklyn with his wife and son.